THE WORKING FOREST
OF BRITISH COLUMBIA

In commemoration
of your
Vancouver Island Tour
February, 1996

Natural Resources Canada

THE WORKING

OF

No natural feature so dominates the geography of
British Columbia as its forests. Shown here is a diverse
landscape of natural and harvested forests near Kamloops
in the interior of the province.

FOREST
BRITISH COLUMBIA

The Working Forest Project
Gerry Burch, RPF, Director
Art Walker, RPF, Coordinator
Peter A. Robson, Writer

Published by Harbour Publishing for I.K. Barber, RPF

Harbour Publishing
P.O. Box 219
Madeira Park, BC, Canada V0N 2H0

Cover, maps, page design and composition by Roger Handling/Terra Firma Design
Illustration page 30 Sean Murphy, all others by Roger Handling.
Front cover photo by Gordon Fisher.
Printed and Bound in Canada

Canadian Cataloguing in Publication Data

Robson, Peter A.
The working forest of British Columbia

Includes index.
ISBN 1-55017-116-X

1. Logging—British Columbia. 2. Logging—British Columbia—Pictorial works. 3. Forests and Forestry—British Columbia. 4. Forests and forestry—British Columbia—Pictorial works.
SD538.3.C2R62 1994   634.9'8'09711   C94-910751-4

Photo credits: 83, 84(b), 111, 113(d), 134(a), 136(a), 137(c), Rick Blacklaws; 113(c), Mark Bostwick; 96(a, b), 97(b, c), 134(b), 135(a, b), 136(b), 137(a, b), 138-39(a, b, c), Ken Bowen; 13, 16(b), 69, 78, 116, 117, British Columbia Archives and Records Service; 46(b, c), 48(a, b), 49(a, b), 52(b) John Parminter, British Columbia Ministry of Forests; 49(c), Canadian Forest Service; 14-15, 33, City of Vancouver Archives; 79(a) IWA, Wilmer Gold Collection; 70, 113(b), Peter A. Robson; 18, Radarsat International; 97(a), 113(a), 138-39(d), 140, 149, Murphy Shewchuk; 31, 32, 41, Keith Thirkell; 15, 19, 33, University of British Columbia Library, Special Collections; 16, 17a, 17b, 27, 51, Vancouver Public Library. All others by the Working Forest Project.

Contents

PLANTED 1953
2 YEAR OLD TREES 8 x 6
PLANTED TREES/ACRE 857
NATURAL TREES/ACRE 30
TOTAL TREES/ACRE 887

MacMillan
Bloedel Limited

Foreword

Many senior British Columbia foresters, myself included, have had the experience of returning to view sites we helped to harvest in earlier times under forest practices that were different than those of today—and have been pleased to find these old sites covered in vibrant new forests.

It is with this in mind that *The Working Forest of British Columbia* was undertaken: to take readers on a "before and after" tour of provincial timber lands to demonstrate that the forests throughout British Columbia have very strong regenerative abilities and have, in fact, established strong, healthy second generation forests both after harvesting and after major disruptions such as fires and windstorms. It is not the purpose of this book to create controversy, nor is it the purpose to defend or criticize the forest harvesting practices that have developed over time. The history of harvesting practices in British Columbia has been driven by technical, economic, and social values, and as these values continue to change so will our management and harvesting practices. However, through all of this, the capacity of our forests to grow and produce new generations of trees is impressive, and most promising for the future.

While *The Working Forest* was intended to explore this process with the reader, two things became clear. First, to demonstrate the story of our changing forests as it has unfolded all across our complex province proved an enormous undertaking—perhaps too challenging for one book. Nevertheless, we have tried to make our coverage as com-

plete as space would allow. Second, The Forest Practices Code and The Forest Renewal Plan, which were being introduced into the planning and management of our forests as this book was being produced, will profoundly affect the future of British Columbia forests, both by recognizing a multitude of other values in addition to timber, and by recognizing the potential to produce greater volumes of fibre per hectare. It is difficult to set down on paper a view of this changing scene that is truly representative in these rapidly changing times.

The Working Forest is also about managing and harvesting our forests by "looking in both directions"—looking backward to learn from the experiences of the past, and looking forward to assure the values and valid demands of the future will be met. It will be for the current generation of foresters, as well as others, to meet these challenges and realize these opportunities.

I wish to express deep appreciation to Mr. Gerry Burch and his many associates, who undertook the creation of *The Working Forest of British Columbia* from its inception to this finished book — thank you, Gerry.

I. K. Barber, RPF

Vigorous second-growth on Vancouver Island forty years after being planted under the direction of forester I.K. Barber.

ACKNOWLEDGEMENTS

Sometime in early 1994 my old friend Ike Barber called me up and told me about an idea which had occurred to him visiting one of the coastal Douglas fir plantations he'd overseen while working as a professional forester in the 1950s. The seedlings he'd planted were now towering high over his head and he couldn't help feeling a surge of pride. From the contemporary viewpoint, the forest management techniques of those earlier times was wanting in many ways, and yet, as millions of hectares of healthy second-growth throughout the province were there to show, the techniques had worked better than they were getting credit for. Ike thought if more people could share the experience of actually viewing the proud young trees they might come to a better understanding of the forest management approach which foresters like ourselves had been administering for the past half century, and he wondered if photographing the new forest and publishing the photos in a book might be an effective way for the public to share that experience.

I had often had similar thoughts, and eagerly agreed to bring Ike's idea into being. Thus the Working Forest Project began. My first move was to enlist the able assistance of Art Walker, a forester I had worked with in industry and who is now a private forestry consultant. Then we assembled a group of fellow foresters, engineers and other forest professionals to map out an approach. We acquired a publisher and together spent the summer of 1994 criss-crossing British Columbia with a team of photographers documenting the working forest and interviewing dozens of men and women who manage it. The result of our efforts was a library of over 10,000 images comprising the most extensive photographic record available of today's working forest, and forming the heart of the book, *The Working Forest of British Columbia*. Space does not permit mention of all who gave so generously of their time to make The Working Forest Project a success, but we hope the list below includes the principal contributors.

W.G. Burch

THE WORKING FOREST PROJECT

Gerry Burch, Director
Art Walker, Coordinator
Pem van Heek, Adviser
Peter A. Robson, Writer

Contributors

Grant Ainscough, Kim Allan, Dave Basaraba, Web Binion, Hubert Bunce, Jim Burbee, Randy Chan, Stan Chester, Don Clutterham, Don Couch, John Deal, Bruce Devitt, Jack Dryburgh, Bill Dumont, Roger Freeman, David Handley, Vic Heath, Bob Helfrich, Trevor Jeanes, Dr. Hamish Kimmins, Keith King, Dick Kosick, Les Laithwaite, Fred Lowenberger, Archie McDonald, Jim MacFarlane, Bill Moore, Patrick Moore, John Murray, Erica Nicholson, John Parminter, Glen Patterson, Ken Pendergast, Sven Rasmussen, Jack Raven, David Raven, John Revel, Bob Richards, Douglas Rickson, Gabriela Sartisohn, Ralph Schmidt, Don Smith, Fred Stinson, Ken Thomas, Steve Tolnai, Allan Van Sickle, Les Skaalid, Gordon Weetman, George von Westarp, Tom Wright.

Special thanks to

Doug Adderley, Chris Fletcher, Matt Hughes, Gary Johansen, Heather Lait, Andy MacKinnon, Peter Murphy, Bill Rosenburg, Craig Roessler, J.C. Scrivener, Rick Slaco, Roxanne Smith, Winston Wai, Rob Woodside.

Project photographers

Zbigniew Olak, Gordon Fisher, Rob Salmon

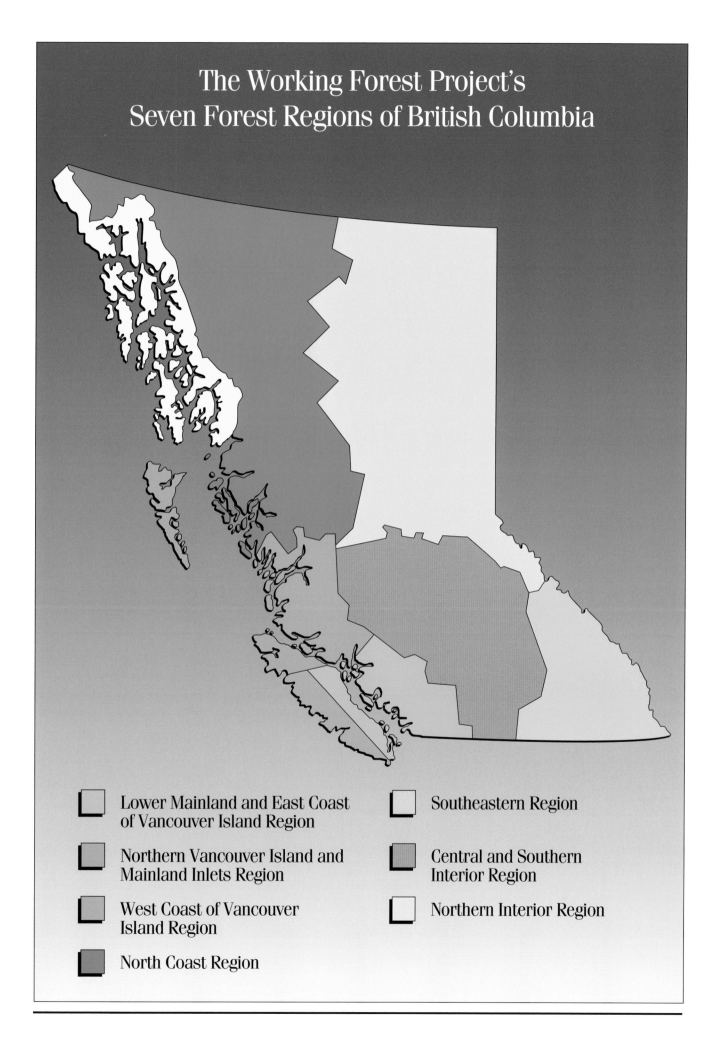

The Working Forest Project's
Seven Forest Regions of British Columbia

Lower Mainland and East Coast of Vancouver Island Region

Northern Vancouver Island and Mainland Inlets Region

West Coast of Vancouver Island Region

North Coast Region

Southeastern Region

Central and Southern Interior Region

Northern Interior Region

PART ONE

At Issue: Sustainable Forestry or "Deforestation"?

No natural feature so dominates the geography of Canada's westernmost province as its forests, an ocean of conifer green surging from the northwestern US through 1,600 kilometres of rainswept coastal fjords, sunburnt interior plateaus and snowy northlands and tundra. Its small, coastal fringe of temperate rain forest is one of the earth's biological treasures. Only one-fifth of 1 percent of the planet's land surface was originally covered in temperate rain forest, and fully two-thirds of that is located here on the northwest coast of North America. In total, the British Columbia forest covers an area greater than France. It is not only a great natural wonder but also a fabulously rich renewable resource.

No human occupants of the region would long endure without coming to terms with the forest. The First Nations of the Pacific Northwest shaped their culture around the overwhelming presence of trees just as surely as the culture of the Polynesians was shaped by the sea. Aboriginal dwellings were constructed of planks and boughs and for transportation they used canoes carved from trees. Their much-celebrated ceremonial art—from the tiny, exquisite shaman's charms of the Sto:lo to the magnificent totem poles of the Haida—was all made from wood. In that they used trees for their material needs, the forest of the first peoples was very much a working forest.

When settlers began coming to the area from Europe

≺ The trackless "sea of mountains" that makes up British Columbia is unsuitable for growing almost everything except trees, but when it comes to trees, it is one of the finest growing sites in North America. Shown here, second growth in the Port Alberni area of Vancouver Island.

No people could survive long in British Columbia without coming to terms with the trees. Native Indians became the first loggers, harvesting trees for shelter, transportation and ceremonial purposes.

in the mid-1800s, they brought with them their Old World preference for open fields, food crops and livestock. They viewed the forest mainly as an obstacle to be cleared away so they could tame the land for grazing and agriculture. Many pioneers spent their days locked in a losing struggle with stubborn stumps, relentless undergrowth and thin soil before they were eventually forced into the realization that still serves as the main justification for the province's working forest. That is, apart from a few select river valleys, deltas and dry grass plateaus comprising less than 5 percent of the province, the trackless "sea of mountains" that makes up British Columbia is unsuitable for growing almost everything except trees.

As the realization sunk in that the timber was a more valuable crop than anything the settlers could hope to replace it with, the commercial harvest of British Columbia's forests began in earnest. In the late 1860s, sawmills appeared on southern Vancouver Island and the Lower Mainland. By 1900, forest harvesting was the province's leading industry—and it has never relinquished

that position. In 1993, it employed 276,000 British Columbians directly and indirectly. British Columbia alone accounted for over 70 percent of Canada's exports of sawn lumber and over half of Canada's total export of forest products. The forest industry is one arena in which British Columbia is unquestionably a world leader.

It is this very success that has placed the forest industry at the centre of a controversy about its impact on the British Columbia forest, which by the 1990s had overflowed provincial boundaries and attracted worldwide attention. Concerns about running out of merchantable timber in British Columbia date back almost to the turn of the century, as do concerns about the effect of large-scale harvesting on fish and game. Conflicts between government logging policies and local groups who wanted to preserve favoured areas also date back to early times, but escalated markedly in the 1970s, 1980s and 1990s with high-profile campaigns to stop logging on Meares Island, the Nitinat Triangle, the Valhalla Wilderness, South Moresby Island, the Carmanah Valley and Clayoquot Sound, among others. All concerns

By 1900 lumbering was the province's leading industry and the principal factor in Vancouver's rise to international prominence. Here, large-dimension structural timbers—the early specialty of coastal mills— are loaded aboard a sailing ship bound for US markets.

As the realization sunk in that the timber was a more valuable crop than anything settlers could hope to replace it with, the commercial harvest of British Columbia's forests began in earnest. The town of Chemainus grew up around this sawmill (below).

Steam power galvanized the harvesting of coastal old growth in the early years of the century. Donkeys, steam-powered winches mounted on large log sleighs, were used to pull timber out of the forest. Here, an early steam donkey is being moved via railcar.

*(Left) A spar tree is topped in the early 1900s. High-lead
logging, using elaborately rigged wooden spars (above) to drag
logs more readily over the ground, completed the
technology that made British Columbia's forest industry
a world leader by the time of the Second World War.*

◄ *A locomotive specially geared for logging duty pulls a trainload of
prime Douglas fir in 1926. The impact of large-scale mechanization
gave rise to concerns about the future of British Columbia's coastal
forests over fifty years ago.*

about the forest industry combined into one heated debate
involving a range of issues from land use to forest management to industrial strategy to environmental pollution.

The war of words and images has continued to seesaw
back and forth without a clear resolution. In the early
1990s, the provincial government lessened tension between
forest policy and its critics by protecting large areas of forest
in the Tatshenshini, Khutzeymateen, Kitlope and other
watersheds, and by proclaiming a new Forest Practices Code
and Forest Renewal program, while remaining committed to
an active working forest as the main engine of the provincial economy.

Debate over the best use of British Columbia's forest
resource has become almost as complex as the ecology of the
forests themselves. Some view the forest as an irreplaceable
natural wonder which should be left undisturbed. Even
when adherents of this view advocate "responsible" harvesting practices, such as partial cutting, they still tend to
view every tree cut as an environmental calamity and every
disturbance of the ecological status quo as an offence to
nature. No amount of wilderness preservation or logging
regulation will make timber extraction acceptable to people
who hold this view because they reject the idea that humanity has any business disturbing the natural order of the forest.

level of ecological disturbance is acceptable, as long as it is reasonable. One of the major worldwide concerns about British Columbia forest practices is rooted in the belief that the scale of harvesting in the province is out of control. The single image which has proven most effective in turning opinion against forest policies, among its supporters as well as its detractors, is the endlessly repeated image of large clearcuts, like the examples of Mount Paxton on northern Vancouver Island, which was once held up to world censure in *National Geographic* magazine, and the sprawling clearcut in the Bowron watershed in the central British Columbia interior, which is said to be visible from space. The criticisms also implied that these areas suffered huge soil losses and that they would never grow trees again.

Except to point out that abolitionists generally fail to realize how much disturbance is natural in British Columbia's forests, *The Working Forest of British Columbia* does not attempt to answer their concerns. This book is directed to the larger segment of the public which accepts the idea that part of the province's sprawling land mass should contain a "working forest," a timber production area where some

A wall poster very popular in college dorms around North America in the early 1990s displayed a large Vancouver Island clearcut captioned by the quote from Shakespeare: "Pardon me thou bleeding piece of earth that I am meek and gentle with these butchers." A forester can look at the same picture and not be offended, because he or she would realize this depicts only one phase of the forest

The single image which has proven most disturbing to the public are frequently repeated pictures of large clearcuts like Mount Paxton on northern Vancouver Island (top), and the Bowron watershed in the central interior (in boxed area of the satellite image at right).

No human occupant of the region would long endure without coming to terms with the forest.

management cycle. Critics characterize the kind of logging carried out in British Columbia clearcutting not as proper forest management but as "liquidation of the forest," as if logging in British Columbia were a one-way road leading to deforestation of large areas of the province; and on the surface the words appear to fit the picture.

Environmentalist Colleen McCrory issued a broadside in 1992 pronouncing British Columbia "the Brazil of the North," vividly tying the images of apparent forest destruction at sites like Mount Paxton and the Bowron Lakes to examples of tropical deforestation in the Amazon rain forest of Brazil.

Those interested in other forest values such as recreation, fish, wildlife and biodiversity naturally assume that if so little thought is being given to basic principles of forest management, non-timber interests could expect even less. Even among those who support the concept of the working forest, there may be a persistent belief that British Columbia is being logged in a manner that degrades growing sites and

destroys the sustainability of the forest resource. There is no doubt that harvesting practices are under intense scrutiny, and demands for change are regularly heard. The question is, is wholesale change justified?

It is this central issue that we intend to examine in this book. Foresters generally deny the charges of irresponsible forest management, but because they are considered partisan, few members of the public are willing to accept their opinions at face value. Certainly Dr. Egon Klepsch, President of the European Parliament, was in no position to do so, which is why he decided to make a tour of British Columbia's forests in March 1993. The effect was decisive. "Your work on environmental issues should be a model for Europe," he told his hosts after the tour. "I had no idea of the extent of the environmental work you've been doing here. I was very surprised, and that is because we are being misinformed [in Europe]."

Few people will have the opportunity to tour the working forest of British Columbia with the thoroughness

SOUTHEAST INTERIOR, COYOTE HILL MID-1970s

A mid-1970s clearcut near Cranbrook in the interior of the province is compared to the same site (right), naturally re-established in native pine and spruce in 1994. The Working Forest Project photographed sites in all parts of British Columbia to examine the effects of commercial harvesting.

permitted a European president, or to talk to the men and women who actually direct forest operations across the province. That is where *The Working Forest of British Columbia* comes in. The brainchild of veteran forester and forest company executive Ike Barber, the Working Forest Project began its work in the summer of 1994, deploying a team of photographers under the direction of senior foresters Gerry Burch and Art Walker to capture the actual state of every major forest region of British Columbia from the air and from the ground. The result is a collection of 10,000 photographs representing the most current and comprehensive visual record of British Columbia's forests presently in existence. In an attempt to give readers everything that can be learned from an actual visit to the working forest, a representative sample of this pictorial record is presented on the following pages.

A two-dimensional view of the forest necessarily has limitations compared with what Dr. Klepsch saw on his tour, but *The Working Forest of British Columbia* has an added dimension even he never experienced—the dimension of time. Time is the crucial missing factor in the image the world has formed of British Columbia's working forest. In the popular mind, Mount Paxton will remain forever frozen in that moment in 1995 when the *National Geographic* photographer snapped his photo of a brown and treeless clearcut. The real mountain, in the meantime, is covered with a new green forest. Forests are as much creatures of time as of space, changing from moment to moment; and no forest, especially no young forest, looks today as it did last year or ten years ago. To begin understanding forest issues is to break through the time barrier and see the forest as a forester sees it—not as a static composition, but as a process of interaction between the growing site and passing time. A forester doesn't see the falling of a tree as the end of

SOUTHEAST INTERIOR, COYOTE HILL 1994

VANCOUVER ISLAND, MOHUN LAKE 1948

A clearcut half a century later. These comparative photos show what few people but foresters ever see: the transformation of a growing site over time. This coastal second-growth stand (right) flourishes in an area that was harvested and slash burned forty-six years earlier.

a story, but as the beginning of the next chapter in an unending story of the growing site as it cycles through time. Removal of a whole stand of trees, whether by fire, disease, wind, insect infestation or clearcutting, is likewise only a note in the symphony of change that is a forest. A clearcut is only a clearcut the day it is cut. The next day it busies itself regrowing a forest.

To give a sense of time's effects, *The Working Forest of British Columbia* has assembled an extensive series of archive photos in which contemporary stands are compared with the same sites at different stages in the forest management cycle. To interpret this unprecedented photographic record, the Working Forest Project worked with and interviewed dozens of professional foresters, engineers and technicians.

Admittedly the view one receives from taking this guided tour of the province is that of the working forest, interpreted by people who work in it, believe in what they do and are proud of their accomplishments. One may or may not come away, as Dr. Klepsch did, feeling that one has seen enough to make up one's mind, but no intelligent position can be taken on the larger forest management issues without first gaining a thorough understanding of conditions as they presently exist. That is what this book hopes to provide.

VANCOUVER ISLAND, MOHUN LAKE 1994

PART TWO

A landscape of old growth and second growth at Carnation Creek
on the west coast of Vancouver Island. The Coastal Western Hemlock
zone—British Columbia's true temperate rain forest—comprises
the low and mid-elevation forests of the coast.

The Evolution of Forest Policy

Most of the early logging activity in British Columbia was concentrated in the populated southwest corner of the province. This has had several important effects on the industry. For one thing, it made the majority of people close witnesses to the effects of large-scale logging, heightening public awareness of forest issues—and not only in recent years. As early as 1918 the Commission of Conservation found "hand-loggers have destroyed the timber on over 1,000 miles of shoreline..." and recommended handlogging be banned as "inimical to the object of forest conservation." In 1910, the government was already sufficiently concerned to hold the first of four royal commissions of inquiry into forest practices. The Fulton Commission's report led to the first inventory of the province's forests and the establishment of the British Columbia Forest Service, responsible for developing and enforcing better forest practices. The future lumber baron H.R. MacMillan, then an idealistic young forestry graduate from Yale, was appointed the province's first chief forester in 1912 and began instituting rudimentary forest management techniques in the British Columbia woods. From this early start, forest practices improved slowly but steadily.

Much of British Columbia's forest policy evolved in response to lessons learned the hard way, a process which continues to this day. Up until 1938 loggers were permitted to leave their wood waste or slash on the ground behind them. In that year, fearing widespread wildfires, the Forest Service mandated that all new logging slash on the east coast of Vancouver Island and the Lower Mainland be burned to reduce the fire hazard. The legislation, however, was too late to prevent a massive fire that ignited many years of accumulated slash on the east coast of Vancouver Island near Campbell River and consumed 32,500 hectares of both slash and forest.

During the Great Depression, high-grading—removing only the most valuable Douglas fir and western red cedar—was the only way logging companies survived. As long as timber supplies appeared endless, such practices

In the Lower Mainland and the east coast of Vancouver Island, harvesting took place in the immediate neighbourhood of the pioneer mills, using teams of oxen and later, horses, to drag logs along greased skid roads to the water.

◄ *Prime old growth on a tributary of the Nimpkish River drainage on northern Vancouver Island, still untouched seven decades after logging began in the valley.*

attracted little criticism, but when people began contemplating the end of the great Douglas fir forests in the late 1930s and 1940s, government became increasingly concerned. It was at this juncture that the provincial chief forester of the day, a man with the wonderfully appropriate name of C.D. Orchard, began to reorganize the wild forests of British Columbia into what he envisioned as one big tree farming operation. Working closely with the Sloan Royal Commission of 1945, Orchard obtained permission to establish new forest practices according to the principles of "sustained yield," whereby future harvesting would be regulated to match the rate at which the forest replaced itself. The industry would be assigned an "Allowable Annual Cut" (AAC), a harvest quota aimed at assuring timber was being harvested no faster than it was growing. This new control on cutting was coupled with a new emphasis on silviculture aimed at restocking logged lands and improving yields.

The doctrine of sustained yield was firmly rooted in traditional European forestry as imported to North America by such pioneer teachers as Bernhard Fernow and studied by H.R. MacMillan before he became British Columbia's chief forester. According to that teaching, the forest was viewed mainly as a growing site for producing timber in the most efficient manner possible, with little recognition of non-timber values. The approach copied agricultural practice. Natural stands of mixed ages and species were to be removed as completely as possible and replaced with a managed crop of the most desirable timber-producing species, which would be cultivated until the stands passed the point of most productive growth. They would then be harvested and another crop rotation started.

Uniformity of age was seen as an advantage, allowing for more efficient management and harvesting. In the old forests, much growing space was taken up by either decadent trees long past their most productive years or immature trees of small size and lower value, both of which were felled and left on the ground after logging. In a stand managed under sustained yield principles, all trees begin growing at the same time, receive the same silvicultural treatments, mature at the same time, and can be harvested in one clean, efficient sweep which adapts well to mechanization. The practice of harvesting all the stems in a stand at one time the way a farmer harvests a crop of wheat, so that the crop can be replanted in the same efficient manner, is central to most traditional European forest management and has been adopted by many forest nations in the world, not just in British Columbia.

Orchard's vision was that if the whole British Columbia forest could be managed under sustained yield principles, the industry would be stabilized and the future of

Conscientious planting activities have had a positive effect on the regeneration of logged or salvaged parts of the forest. The foreground in this photo shows salvaged and replanted slopes near Sproat Lake, while the ridge crest displays unsalvaged snags which are remnants of a large fire.

the province's leading industry would be secure. Sustained yield methods filtered down through the forest industry gradually. First, new tenures (harvesting rights) had to be established to maintain continuity and production levels. Forest Licences were established for approximately 60 percent of the provincial allowable cut, mainly in the interior, and including operators who formerly depended on timber sales for logs for their sawmills. Tree Farm Licences (TFLs) were granted for approximately 25 percent of the cut, mainly to larger companies with private timber holdings and higher volume demands. Later, the Small Business Forest Enterprise Program was initiated to make timber available to smaller operators. With this latter tenure, the Forest Service would be responsible for planning, road construction, site preparation and reforestation. All of these tenures are controlled by allowable annual cut levels as established by the provincial chief forester.

Greater emphasis shifted to the future crop, and loggers were required to remove all merchantable wood from a site so that it could be reforested—on the coast this was mainly by planting. In this way the silviculture system known as "clearcutting" became established as the industry standard in British Columbia for both silvicultural and economic reasons. Planting nursery seedlings grown from seed collected near the harvested area became standard practice in the sixties and seventies, but through the forties and fifties the only silvicultural treatment was to bare the ground for natural seeding by burning the slash, particularly on the lower coast.

Returning forty, sixty and eighty years later to view logged land, one notices immediately how well the forest has rebounded under all treatments—even no treatment at all. Much of the most successful second growth was seeded by nature with no help from foresters. In the 1960s and 1970s Douglas fir was the only nursery stock produced; it was planted extensively on the coast, but experience showed that areas which originally supported western hemlock or western red cedar often did so for good reason.

In the late 1960s, Dr. Vladimir Krajina, professor of botany at the University of British Columbia, introduced the concept of identifying forest ecosystems based on a biogeoclimatic classification system. This world-renowned system combines similar segments of a forest ecosystem by analyzing vegetation, soil, topography and climate. Biogeoclimatic zones are named after one or more of the dominant tree species found on the site and can be further broken into subzones based on narrower climatic variations. This classification system is now required on all sites planned for harvest in British Columbia according to the Silviculture Regulations (1988), and it spells out the most compatible species to be established after harvesting. Today, forest industry nurseries produce eighteen different species and plantings are varied according to site. During the 1960s, one of the effects of improved inventories and higher utilization standards was that the Forest Service increased

Allowable Annual Cuts. In 1992, however, primarily due to land extractions, the province's chief forester John Cuthbert ordered the AAC lowered in some management units. Others were less affected. Forester Gerry Burch believes that there is much misunderstanding surrounding the subject of AACs. He notes that the calculation of AACs is not an exact science and is still open to debate.

"The chief forester reviews AACs every five years and numerous factors are incorporated into those calculations," explains Burch. "They include: extraction of productive forest lands for other uses, new data on growth rates, inclusion of operable timber stands that were formerly inaccessible, changing utilization standards, and losses due to major forest fires or insect attacks." Allowable annual cuts may increase or decrease because of these factors, but Burch notes that forest companies have always harvested what Forest Service regulations required. Overcutting or undercutting, in the sense of exceeding prescribed government limits, did not occur without permission. Burch stresses, "Strict government regulations and penalties govern any deviance from the calculated AAC, either on an annual or 5-year basis." Among foresters, opinion remains divided on whether the AAC should be lowered further, or raised. Some believe timber supplies will diminish once all the working forest's economically accessible and available old growth is cut and the industry finds itself dependent on the smaller second-growth trees—the so-called "falldown" effect. Others believe the new managed crop, benefitting from better reforestation, silvicultural enhancements and higher utilization, could yield higher and better volumes than the wild crop.

Although the term "sustained yield" has fallen out of use in British Columbia's forestry circles in recent years, the concept remains as the basis for the province's approach to forest management. Many revisions have been made, up to and including the introduction of the Forest Practices Code of 1995, but the general thrust of all these revisions has been to broaden the classic sustained yield emphasis on timber production to take account of non-timber values.

As the province became more populated, competition for forest land from ranchers, hunters, fishers, recreationists and others increased, and the Forest Service responded with a new approach called the Multiple Use Strategy. The strategy was adopted in the 1960s by then Chief Forester Bill Young, who instituted a folio system using map overlays to locate areas of conflict among different users of the forest. This trend also spawned new courses in natural resource management at British Columbia's universities, where students learn a broad range of resource management skills in the diverse topics of fisheries, wildlife, range and forestry. Competition for forest land has increased so much in the intervening years that foresters like Trevor Jeanes of Kamloops say they spend more time dealing with non-timber issues than in planning harvesting operations.

THE WORKING FOREST OF BRITISH COLUMBIA

Endless as they may seem from the window of an aircraft, the forests of British Columbia cover only 59 million of the province's 95 million hectares. Of the forested portion, over 33 million hectares are set aside for parks, wilderness reserves and land use classes other than forestry. Touching every region of the province, these protected sites are as large as the combined area of England and Scotland, giving British Columbia one of the biggest preserved forest areas to be found anywhere in the world. This area of preserved forest has increased significantly in recent years and continues to expand.

One of the central questions raised about the working forest is whether or not it is the best use of the land it occupies. In this context it is useful to look closely at just how much land it does use. Of the 59 million hectares of forest land in British Columbia, 46 million hectares are considered productive. The working forest—the area dedicated to growing harvestable and merchantable timber—makes up 26 million hectares, or slightly over one-quarter of the total area of British Columbia. Of this, however, over 90 percent is always free of active logging and available for a wide range of non-industrial uses—especially recreation. In any given year, less than 1 percent of the working forest land base—an average of 224,000 hectares—is subject to forest harvesting activities.

When looking at the working forest and considering arguments that British Columbia forest policy errs in placing too much value on timber production and not enough on non-timber values such as recreation, wildlife and biodiversity, it is important to keep in mind there is a larger tract of forest land where timber production has no status whatever, and non-timber values are paramount. For many years it was considered that this vast tract of preserved forest principally fulfilled non-timber needs, leaving the working forest free to pursue timber values, but recently wood production has been increasingly giving way to other uses, even in the working forest.

The Forests of British Columbia

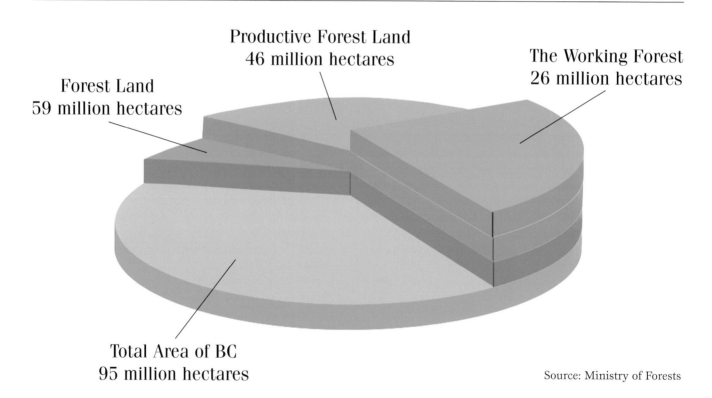

Productive Forest Land
46 million hectares

The Working Forest
26 million hectares

Forest Land
59 million hectares

Total Area of BC
95 million hectares

Source: Ministry of Forests

Ocean and Rain Forest: The Coastal Forests

ritish Columbia's coastal forests carpet Vancouver Island and the Queen Charlotte Islands and span the length of the mainland coast inland to the Coast Mountains. Almost all of the area is mountainous. The Alpine Tundra is found at higher elevations of the Coast Range and supports only dwarf trees and shrubs, herbs, lichens and mosses. The Mountain Hemlock zone is predominant on the middle to high elevations. In this band of forest, mountain hemlock and balsam are the dominant species and varying amounts of yellow cedar also occur. The Coastal Western Hemlock zone—British Columbia's true temperate rain forests—comprise the lower elevation forests along the coastal fringe and the shores of most coastal inlets. Western hemlock and balsam are the dominant trees. Western red cedar, Sitka spruce and yellow cedar are found on wetter sites in this area and can live to great ages. In contrast, the drier, leeward slopes and valleys of the coast are home to almost pure stands of Douglas fir. There are great variations in forest types within the narrow band of coastal forest, and in this section we will look at three distinct zones: the Lower Mainland and east coast of Vancouver Island, northern Vancouver Island, and the west coast of Vancouver Island.

A landscape typical of British Columbia's coastal forests.

The Douglas Fir Forests: East Coast of Vancouver Island and the Lower Mainland

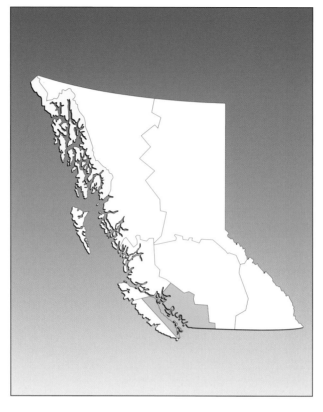

In the province's more populated southwest corner, including the Lower Mainland, the Sunshine Coast and the southeast portion of Vancouver Island, virtually every square metre was once blanketed in heavy temperate rain forest up to the timberline. Most of the rainfall that sweeps in from the Pacific Ocean falls on the windward, or western slopes of Vancouver Island, giving it the highest measured precipitation in Canada. In contrast, the southeast coast of the Island and the Lower Mainland are in the rainshadow, or leeward side. This region comprises what is known as the Coastal Douglas fir biogeoclimatic zone. The comparatively drier climate and productive soils combined to provide a forest ecosystem that supported one of the most magnificent forests in the world. Douglas fir is capable of growing to great age without deteriorating and some coastal old-growth stands averaged over 400 years, producing giant trees which reached heights nearing 120 metres. These huge trees produced lumber renowned around the world for its strength and great dimensions, vying with steel as the pre-

ferred framing material for large buildings during the first decades of the century.

Douglas fir is by far the most common species in this zone. However, it shares the wetter sites with grand fir, western red cedar, western hemlock, red alder and bigleaf maple, while arbutus and shore pine may be found on drier sites. The southern tip of Vancouver Island once had a unique landscape of Garry oak woodland, on which settlement was and is having a severe impact.

Although 70 percent of British Columbia's modern timber harvest comes from the interior of the province, lumbering developed first on the south coast, and for the first century, the lower coastal region was where all the logging took place. In the 1990s, many of those early communities continue to rely on the forest industry as a major source of revenue. They include Mission, Squamish, Lillooet, Powell River, Campbell River, Port Alberni, Ladysmith, Lake Cowichan, Duncan and the Hope-Fraser Canyon and Sunshine Coast areas. Commercial cutting in the region began with the establishment of

This magnificent stand of Douglas fir old-growth in the Upper Elaho River valley illustrates the value of major forest disturbances such as wildfire or clearcut logging. Because the Douglas fir does not germinate in the cool, dark soil of the old-growth forest, these aging giants are being replaced by smaller and less valuable western hemlock, which thrives in the shade. Douglas fir can regenerate on such a site only if a major disturbance opens the canopy, allows sunlight in and warms the soil.

Commercial cutting on British Columbia's south coast began in the 1860s, and spread outward from the population centres of Vancouver and Victoria.
(Left) A Douglas fir seedling regenerates in a clearcut.
(Top) Early fallers use axes and saws to fall a western red cedar.
(Below) Prime Douglas fir logs are loaded onto railcars.

the earliest mills in the 1860s and spread outward from the population centres of Vancouver and Victoria, moving through the prime old-growth Douglas fir northward along the mainland coast and up the east coast of Vancouver Island. In the beginning, harvesting took place in the immediate neighbourhood of the pioneer mills, using teams of oxen and later horses to drag logs to the water. Log supplies were supplemented by handloggers, lone operators who spread out along the inlets falling prime shorefront trees into the sea where they could be floated to the mills. New markets kept opening for the large-dimension structural timbers that were the early specialty of coastal mills, and demand for new stands of choice old-growth Douglas fir grew rapidly in the early years of the century. By 1910 steam

logging was established in the province, spawning railway camps the size of small towns as far north as the Nimpkish Valley on Vancouver Island. Log production shot up to 1 billion board feet a year and began biting deeply into the coastal Douglas fir forest. By the Second World War the biggest valleys had been worked and the glory days of the steam era were fading. Many felt logging itself was on the downslope, with the end of the towering old-growth Douglas fir stands in sight.

What people failed to anticipate was how profoundly new technology would combine with increased demand to keep bringing previously unmerchantable and inaccessible timber into the merchantable category, continually expanding the timber supply across the province. At the beginning

SPROAT LAKE, VANCOUVER ISLAND 1978

The old-growth Douglas fir forest on this mountainside adjacent to Sproat Lake was consumed in 1967, not by logging, but by the 7,000 hectare Taylor River forest fire. Such fires were typical of the dry Douglas fir region before modern fire-fighting technology was developed. Following the fire, snags were felled and Douglas fir was planted in the easily accessible areas. In 1994, the area had regenerated well. Snags in the brown areas of the photo were left standing following the fire and regeneration was natural.

SPROAT LAKE, VANCOUVER ISLAND 1994

WIDOW CREEK, VANCOUVER ISLAND 1985

This site at Widow Creek near Cowichan Lake was harvested in 1979. The photo was taken in 1985. Web Binion, forest supervisor, was in charge of the logging, slash burning and planting.

WIDOW CREEK, VANCOUVER ISLAND 1994

"The working forest is being renewed, and in the majority of cases the yearly growth can be increased through good management."
Web Binion, *forest supervisor.*

of the Second World War, the emergence of truck logging opened up higher-elevation stands which were too steep for the railways to reach. During both world wars, the aviation industry created a sudden demand for Sitka spruce. The growth of the pulp industry created a demand for hemlock and balsam, and much later, for western red cedar. Kiln-drying allowed hemlock to be exported as lumber. Plywood created new applications and opened new markets for British Columbia wood products. Various types of composition board created uses for previously discarded by-products. Improved mill technology allowed small-diameter logs to be sawn for lumber. Western red cedar became popular as a decorative feature in home construction. Loggers found themselves returning to harvest stands they'd previously passed by, and re-logging settings to take out trees left behind on the first pass. No longer restricted to prime old-growth Douglas fir of the south coast, the industry spread out across the province, tackling vast tracts of timber on the north coast and in the interior which had previously been considered unmerchantable.

While in 1995 most of the province's forest districts retained the bulk of their natural old-growth, southeastern Vancouver Island and the Lower Mainland are unique in the degree to which they have been cut over. Most of the south coast area was logged of its natural forests between the 1860s and 1980s. Initially, much of this timber cutting was done to make way for agriculture. The rich valley bottoms held the most productive soils in the province which were

SAYWARD, VANCOUVER ISLAND 1939

One of British Columbia's large forest fires (32,500 hectares) started in the Sayward area of Vancouver Island in 1938. The lower photo indicates the new forest of planted trees which were juvenile spaced and some portions fertilized.

SAYWARD, VANCOUVER ISLAND 1994

quickly exploited and turned into farmland.

Another major influence occurred in 1885 when almost the entire southeast portion of Vancouver Island (850,000 hectares) was granted to the Esquimalt & Nanaimo Railway Company as concession for the company to establish a railway service on the Island. This private land was later sold to a variety of interests and, because private land was not subject to government regulation, most of that land was rapidly logged. Some of the land was then converted to non-forest uses such as agriculture, townsites, roads, hydro lines or industry. In the 1990s, the areas that were logged, but maintained as forest land, represent not only the largest tracts of forest land on southeast Vancouver Island, but some of the most mature second-growth forests in the province.

Dick Kosick has been a forester for thirty-seven years and is superintendent of planning for Pacific Forest Products Ltd., a company with timber holdings throughout Vancouver Island and the mainland coast, including 109,864 hectares of productive private land on the east coast of Vancouver Island.

Of the 91,000 hectares of forest land the company and its predecessors logged over the past 100 years, Kosick says that 98 percent of that is now growing new forests. "These trees are growing in some of the most productive soils in the world for Douglas fir and they have an amazing ability to grow."

Kosick notes that some of the trees he planted in 1958 are now large enough to harvest. "On some of the better

HEMMINGSEN CREEK, VANCOUVER ISLAND 1974 & 1994

Before and after views, twenty years apart, showing how immediate reforestation on a clearcut and slash-burned area can produce a vigorous new forest with ready road access for recreation. An emphasis on immediate reforestation came about as a result of a sustained yield approach to forestry.

sites, those trees average 40 centimetres," he says, "but I'd hate to see them cut at this stage because they're putting on so much volume."

Kosick is one of those who believe that some second-growth stands will yield volumes equivalent to the average volume of old-growth from the same sites. He estimates that the old-growth stands his company has logged, which had significant waste due to natural damage, rot, disease and mortality, yielded an average of 850 cubic metres per hectare. Kosick reports that some of their second-growth plots, after sixty years, now measure very close to that volume.

Forester Gerry Burch spent most of his career working among the forests of Vancouver Island. Burch notes that stands harvested forty to sixty years ago are now reaching a merchantable size. He says this has opened up new possibilities for commercial thinning in the working forest. This process of removing a portion of the trees both provides merchantable timber and increases the amount of sunlight and moisture available to the remaining trees so that they grow at a faster rate. "There is an increasing trend toward the commercial thinning of these immature stands," explains Burch. "The volume achieved from thinnings will substantially contribute to increased employment, community stability, revenues to government and help stabilize allowable cuts." David Handley is a retired forester who spent his forty-year career on Vancouver Island with MacMillan Bloedel Ltd. He has managed silvicultural research operations all over the coast and studied new

WILSON CREEK, VANCOUVER ISLAND 1973

The trees in this valley suffered a severe insect infestation in the 1940s, which necessitated an immediate salvage operation. Many pioneering silvicultural projects were carried out, resulting in robust second-growth.

WILSON CREEK, VANCOUVER ISLAND 1994

forests as part of his work. He says that not only are the second-growth forests of the east coast of Vancouver Island regenerating well, they are also healthy.

Explains Handley: "Whether seeded naturally or planted, the new forest is growing well. Only a trained eye can detect whether an area was planted or natural. The forests are healthy for the most part, but on some sites a yellow hue in the foliage shows a shortage of nitrogen in the soil, a common failing of the Island's largely glacial soils." Continues Handley: "Root diseases have been inherited from the predecessor, old-growth trees, but despite assertions to the contrary, disease is natural and rare, rather than widespread. Now that the problem is known, infected sites are identified before logging and infected roots and stumps removed and disease-resistant species planted. Management is improving the working forest."

Whether nature or man has started the cycle of renewal of the forests on the east coast of Vancouver Island and the Lower Mainland, new forests have replaced the old. And whether nature has naturally regenerated those stands or man has planted them, there is surprisingly little variation from the historical variety of species. It is the belief of people like Gerry Burch, Dick Kosick and David Handley, who have spent their lives in the woods, that logging in general has compromised neither the health of the stands nor the ability of the ecosystem to reproduce the original forests.

COWICHAN LAKE, VANCOUVER ISLAND, TRUCK ROAD 2 1965

This photo depicts an area which was logged with subsequent slash burning and planting on a steep slope. The trees have grown rapidly and stabilized the slope, thus minimizing erosion and providing for food and cover for the numerous deer in the area.

COWICHAN LAKE, VANCOUVER ISLAND, TRUCK ROAD 2 1994

"Whether seeded naturally or planted, the new forest is growing well. Only a trained eye can detect whether an area was planted or natural."
David Handley, *forester.*

ROBERTSON VALLEY, VANCOUVER ISLAND 1957 & 1994

(Above left) This valley, which was harvested by railway and steam skidders in the 1930s, left big clearcuts which required extensive planting projects in the 1940s and 1950s, mostly by the Forest Service. Forester Bruce Devitt (both photos above) was in charge of this reforestation project.

ROBERTSON VALLEY, VANCOUVER ISLAND 1994

STANLEY PARK & PACIFIC SPIRIT PARK, VANCOUVER, 1994

Many of British Columbia's most popular forested areas were logged in the late 1880s and 1890s and left to regenerate naturally. A hundred years later, such areas as Stanley Park (left), Pacific Spirit Park on the University of British Columbia Endowment Lands (below), and many portions of the North Shore mountains opposite Vancouver, exhibit characteristics of ancient forests.

Kim Allan, chief forester for the Municipality of Mission's Tree Farm Licence, views some excellent regrowth. This municipal forest is widely used for recreation.

"Each year, BC's forests are subject to new regulations that are based on increasing knowledge, as well as greater consideration for public and non-commercial values. We need to reach a balance that reflects an appropriate mix of economic, environmental, sustainable, social and cultural considerations."
Kim Allan, forester.

STAVE LAKE, LOWER MAINLAND 1975

Views of a large clearcut in the 1970s. The harvested area was then burned and planted to local species.

STAVE LAKE, LOWER MAINLAND 1995

MISSION, LOWER MAINLAND 1968

(Left) A slash burn following logging in 1968. (Below) The same site in 1994. Burning logging slash was required in most dry regions of the coast after 1938. The aim was to remove only the fine fuels (twigs, branches, brush) from a cutblock and leave a carbon layer on the large debris to impede wildfire. The procedure also made planting easier. In 1994, slash burning was used on less than 20 percent of the area harvested in the province.

MISSION, LOWER MAINLAND 1994

 ## Nature's Clearcuts:
Natural Disturbances to the Forest Ecosystem

Many people cannot comprehend how a forester steeped in the traditions of forest science could look calmly upon the seemingly catastrophic destruction wrought by a large clearcut. The explanation lies in the differing perceptions about the role of major disturbances in the forest ecosystem. Scientific opinion is anything but unanimous on the question, but most foresters believe that disturbances are natural to most forest ecosystems, and in many cases are essential to their well-being.

Over the past two million years, the climate of the Pacific Northwest has undergone cataclysmic change—at times the area was buried under kilometres of ice, at other times it was lush with tropical forests. Each ice age smoth-

ered the forests for tens of thousands of years, and when the ice sheets withdrew, forests returned to carpet the valleys and mountains for many more thousands of years. The last ice age retreated from the Pacific Northwest only ten thousand years ago—a mere moment in evolutionary time. The apparently ancient forests that carpeted the Pacific Northwest when Europeans first arrived had re-asserted their dominance after being obliterated by the ice only a few dozen forest generations earlier.

This ability to bounce back from drastic upheaval is obviously something nature has built into the forest and can be seen operating on a smaller scale even today. In spite of human attempts to limit their impact, large-scale wildfires,

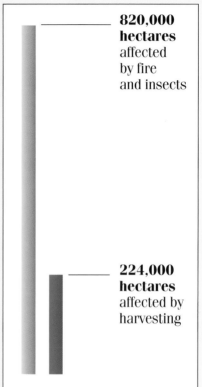

820,000 hectares affected by fire and insects

224,000 hectares affected by harvesting

Large-scale disturbances, where hundreds of hectares of forest are destroyed by fire, windthrow or insects, is a constant occurrence in the natural forest. In the ten-year period between 1984 and 1994, disturbance by fire and insects alone annually affected an average of 820,000 hectares of forest land in British Columbia.

windstorms, landslides and insect infestations annually affect an average of 820,000 hectares of British Columbia's forests—over three and one-half times the amount harvested.

Opinion varies on the role that major disturbance plays in removing overmature trees to make room for new growth—a function essential to forest health. Some argue that under natural conditions the forest typically renews itself one tree at a time, and that it should be harvested using partial cutting systems rather than clearcutting. Others say the notion that nature will always work in the best interests of the forest if left undisturbed is a wishful oversimplification.

A common form of natural regression can be seen in progress at MacMillan Park on Vancouver Island's Parksville–Port Alberni highway, where H.R. MacMillan preserved an impressive stand of giant Douglas fir old-growth known as Cathedral Grove. The ancient trees are deteriorating but tourists can walk among the great trunks for hours and not find a single Douglas fir seedling growing to replace the giants. They will find conifer seedlings by the thousands, but they will prove to be shade-tolerant species such as western hemlock, red cedar, or grand fir. This is because Douglas fir does not germinate well in the cool, shaded soil under a heavy old-growth canopy, while some other species thrive. If left undisturbed, most Douglas fir sites would be dominated by other species. The only thing that allows Douglas fir to regenerate is some form of major

The ability to bounce back from drastic upheaval is obviously something nature has built into the forest. In spite of humanity's attempts to limit their impact, large scale wildfires, windstorms, landslides and insect infestations annually affect almost four times the amount harvested.

(Left) A single lightning storm has been known to produce 10,000 strikes and start more than 300 blazes. Sometimes the fires are limited to small patches, others can burn vast areas.

(Right) The result of a massive wildfire in Kwadacha Wilderness Park in northeastern British Columbia in 1981. Wildfires can burn hundreds of thousands of hectares of forest land. Where accessible, salvage harvesting operations are directed to areas burned by wildfire.

(Bottom) The Allan Creek wildfire in the north Thompson River watershed in the BC interior in 1975.

Despite modern fire-fighting technology, the 1994 Penticton fire burned
5,500 hectares, destroying homes (top) and threatening
urban areas before it was brought under control.
(Bottom) These fire breaks were created in efforts to stop
the spread of the fire.

Over the past two million years, the environment of the Pacific Northwest has undergone cataclysmic change—at times covered under kilometres of ice, at other times, lush with tropical forests. Each ice age smothered the forests for tens of thousands of years, and when the ice sheets withdrew, forests returned to carpet the valleys and mountains for thousands more years.

(Left) This slide followed a 1981 fire in Kwadacha Wilderness Park.

Snow avalanches like the ones shown here on the west side of the Upper Arrow Lakes in the BC interior represent another natural and ongoing disturbance in the mountainous regions that cover much of British Columbia.

disturbance which opens the canopy, lets sunlight in and warms the soil so that the new seedlings of this species can thrive.

Foresters maintain that the very existence of a Douglas fir zone is evidence of the central role played by major disturbances. It is evidence as well of the role that broadcast harvesting techniques can play in maintaining the historic character of coastal forests.

Certainly some species do produce multi-aged stands where the oldest trees die off and are replaced by new seedlings one at a time, but more typically, wildfires have burnt over huge areas of the province's drier zones like clockwork, especially in the British Columbia interior. Just as regularly, insect populations explode and destroy hundreds of thousands of hectares of interior forest.

On the less moist areas of the coast, large-scale wildfire has also been a constant influence. In summer, hot winds blast across the eastern slopes of Vancouver Island where relative humidities sometimes reach explosive levels. Forests are often tinder-dry at the height of summer and a single lightning strike is all it takes to touch off a fire. Before fire-fighting crews and air tankers arrive, it can race through thousands of hectares of the forest unchecked.

On the wetter parts of the coast where fire is less

This blowdown occurred in Tweedsmuir Park in the BC interior in 1991. Similar blowdowns occur continually all over the province. The most extensive blowdowns are caused by hurricanes that visit the outer British Columbia coast every few decades.

(Centre right) A close-up of one of the blowdowns in the photo above. Natural calamities such as this belie the idea the forest ecology is a frail system unable to tolerate disruption.

The lodgepole pine trees in this 1986 photo of the Flathead area were killed by an infestation of mountain pine beetle. In 1984, at the height of the most recent epidemic, the mountain pine beetle infested almost 500,000 hectares of lodgepole pine forest in British Columbia's interior. This is more than double the area annually harvested in the whole province.

frequent, nature seems to have found an alternate way of creating major disturbance in the form of windthrow or blowdown—the levelling of whole stands by strong winds. Many species native to the area have shallow roots which causes the trees to blow over readily, and numerous small blowdowns occur every year. There is also historical evidence of colossal blowdowns—hundreds of times larger than the biggest clearcut—caused by the hurricanes that visit the area every few decades. One of the largest blowdowns in history cut a 10- by 75-kilometre swath across Vancouver Island from Winter Harbour to Port McNeill at the turn of the century. In 1906, following a major storm on the east coast of Vancouver Island, one newspaper reported that a person could walk 25 kilometres from Duncan to Cowichan Lake on fallen timber. In 1921, another storm hit the lower west coast of Vancouver Island and blew down timber for 160 kilometres, as well as 350 square kilometres of forest on the Olympic Peninsula to the south. One of the best remembered storms, Typhoon Frieda, devastated the second-growth forest in Vancouver's Stanley Park and blew down hundreds of square kilometres of timber along the British Columbia coast in October 1962. With this back-ground of natural disturbance, foresters plan timber harvesting with ever increasing attempts to minimize environmental impacts, whereas nature does a poor job of planning. Wildfires occur in the summer when most damage to the soil can result, and blowdown usually occurs in the winter when the soil is saturated with rainfall and the chance of siltation is the highest.

It is clear that large-scale disturbances, where hundreds of hectares of forest are destroyed by fire, windthrow or insects, are constant occurrences in the natural forest. In the 1930s, before government and industry began taking measures to limit them, wildfires alone affected an average of 220,000 hectares per year, roughly equal to the annual harvest of the 1990s.

Whether or not the regular cycle of natural disturbance represents nature's optimum method for renewing the forest depends on who you listen to, but the forests we know are undeniably a product of an endless chain of cataclysmic upheaval stretching back through time. Knowing this, the forester tends to view clearcut openings as consistent with the normal historical experience of the forest.

THE FOREST TOUR

Wind and Weather: The Forests of Northern Vancouver Island and Mainland Inlets

The northern end of Vancouver Island is characterized by gentle, undulating, low-elevation mountains. Farther south, the country rises to become more mountainous and rugged. The adjacent mainland inlets—Bute, Knight, Kingcome and Seymour—are carved deep into the coast and sweep up from the ocean into the snowcapped Coast Mountains. The entire region is rimmed by the mighty Pacific Ocean and carpeted with forests. Rainfall averages 250 to 350 centimetres per year and fierce storms often lash the area. Communities that depend largely on the forest industry include Port McNeill, Port Hardy, Port Alice, Woss and Winter Harbour.

The dominant trees throughout most of the north Island area are western hemlock, balsam and red cedar. However, on the drier eastern portion of the north Island, notably in the Nimpkish Valley, Douglas fir is abundant.

The wet climate protects the north Island from the fires that devastate forests elsewhere in the province, but it has an equally destructive natural force: wind. As a result, the forests on exposed slopes of the north Island have a lower average age and lack the old-growth characteristics found in some of the protected valleys farther south.

The adverse winds that batter the forests of the north Island are also an agent of renewal. Like most coastal species, western hemlock, Sitka spruce and balsam are prolific seed producers. Winged seeds, particularly those of hemlock and spruce, carry long distances on the wind and quickly establish themselves in large numbers in the disturbed soil of a clearing. Before the stand matures, most will lose their fight for light

The dominant trees throughout most of northern Vancouver Island area are western hemlock, balsam and red cedar. However, on the drier eastern portion of the north Island, notably in the Nimpkish Valley, Douglas fir is abundant.

In the Nimpkish Valley on the sheltered eastern slopes of the north Island, the gently rolling terrain and rich Douglas fir forest were well suited to railroad logging.

Veteran forester Tom Wright on British Columbia's last surviving logging railway in the Nimpkish Valley in 1994.

"Clearcutting benefits those species which require full sunlight to become established and survive as young seedlings. The Douglas fir, for example, will not grow in its own shade, except in some of the drier parts of its range. But given the opportunity to grow in the sunlight after the land has been cleared by fire or logging, it produces some of the finest forests in the world."

Tom Wright, professional forester.

and moisture and only a few hundred per hectare will survive to form the mature forest.

This history of massive disturbance followed by abundant regrowth has shown that change is a natural feature of the forest ecosystem on the north Island. Here as elsewhere, the forest demonstrates a powerful regenerative impulse which requires disturbance to thrive.

Early in British Columbia's forest history, the hemlock–balsam forests of the north Island had little value in a market flooded with prime Douglas fir much closer to the mills, so large-scale logging operations in these stands did not get underway until about 1915. At that time, timber harvesting rights to a large portion of the Quatsino Sound area were purchased and a pulp mill was built at Port Alice. For the next forty-five years, most of the western

A small, localized patch of blowdown. Historically, blowdown has served as a significant natural force in the renewal of the forests of the north Island.

WOLFE LAKE, VANCOUVER ISLAND 1955

This Nimpkish Valley block was clearcut to the water's edge in 1955, a practice no longer permitted. In 2040, the second growth visible on this 1955 clearcut will be ready for the second harvest. Although the Nimpkish Valley has been logged longer than any part of Northern Vancouver Island, much old-growth timber remains to be harvested.

WOLFE LAKE, VANCOUVER ISLAND 1994

hemlock and balsam logged in the area was used in the production of pulp.

In the late 1930s, the advent of effective rock drilling machinery and reliable log-hauling trucks extended the logger's reach even higher up the mountains. Also around this time, the innovative Koerner family arrived from Czechoslovakia and developed an export market for kiln-dried western hemlock lumber, creating new demands for the timber of the north Island.

Bill Dumont is the chief forester for Western Forest Products Ltd., successor to the Koerners' company and one of the major forest products firms on the north Island today.

In 1995, Dumont estimated that after eighty years of logging in the Quatsino Sound area, more than half—86,000 hectares—of the 156,000 hectares of productive forest in the company's Tree Farm Licence remains in its natural old-growth state. Of the 70,000 hectares harvested over the years, he calculates that 98 percent now supports new forests. Those second-growth forests, says Dumont, "range from new plantations to magnificent naturally regenerated stands of western hemlock that rate among the finest in the world." The 2 percent of Western's productive forest lands not currently forested, explains Dumont, are made up of roads necessary to access the timber, communities to house

WOSS LAKE, VANCOUVER ISLAND 1951

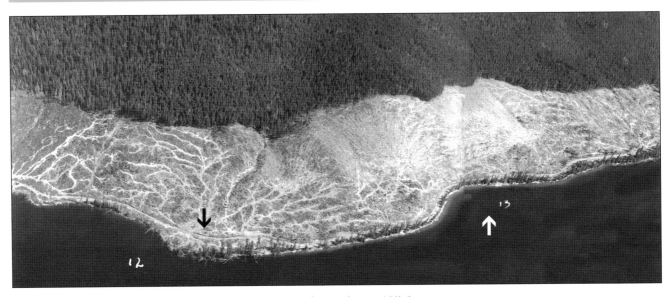

This area in the Nimpkish Valley as well as the Sutton Creek site (opposite) were riddled with roads after being logged by ground traction machines.

WOSS LAKE, VANCOUVER ISLAND 1994

SUTTON CREEK, VANCOUVER ISLAND 1957

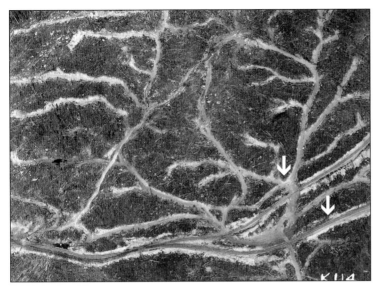

The practice of using dense road systems to bring traction yarding equipment close to the timber has been discontinued in wet coastal areas because of the high impact on forest soils. Despite the apparent damage here, both Woss Lake and Sutton Creek sites were covered in healthy second-growth in 1994. The mainline roads were maintained for fire protection, stand management and public access.

SUTTON CREEK, VANCOUVER ISLAND 1994

Glen Patterson, former area forester in charge of planning for the Nimpkish Valley when the area was harvested.

"If we do not harvest old growth, nature will do the job, as it has over the centuries, with insects, disease, wind and fire. Despite nearly a century of harvesting old-growth forests on Vancouver Island, half remains."
Glen Patterson, forester.

NORTH OF HOOMAK LAKE, VANCOUVER ISLAND 1951

Four decades after cutting, the mixed fir-hemlock-cedar stands north of Hoomak Lake show vigorous regrowth. The Island Highway passes through the centre of the photo (right).

"It is easy for me to feel confident about the future of our second growth, I've been working in the woods for nearly forty years. I can recall driving up the Island Highway years ago and it was all clearcut on both sides and you had a grand view of the mountains. You drive through there now, but you can't see anything. You're going through a 'green tunnel' with trees 12 and 15 metres tall on either side."
Doug Rickson, *former chief forester of Canadian Forest Products.*

NORTH OF HOOMAK LAKE, VANCOUVER ISLAND 1994

forest workers and their families, and freshly logged areas awaiting planting.

Dumont estimates that at current harvest rates, the remaining old-growth scheduled for harvesting will sustain the company until the year 2040. Following that, the forests that regenerated after logging in the early 1900s will be mature and available for harvest, continuing the cycle of crop rotations that should provide timber in perpetuity.

"This is true conservation," stresses Dumont. "What other country in the world has more than half of its original forests left after almost a century of logging? This to me is a testament to pretty responsible forestry."

Farther south, in the Nimpkish Valley on the sheltered eastern slopes of the north Island, the gently rolling terrain and heavy Douglas fir forest were well suited to railway logging. Large-scale operations began in the 1920s when track was laid into the valley from Beaver Cove. When the rails reached 25-kilometre-long Nimpkish Lake, A-frames were

FROST LAKE, VANCOUVER ISLAND 1956

Cutting patterns and regrowth in the Nimpkish Valley. This 1956 photo shows fresh high-lead logging slash in the upper half and slightly older workings done with ground yarding equipment in the lower half. Adjacent old-growth was logged later. Lower photo shows regrowth thirty-six years later.

FROST LAKE, VANCOUVER ISLAND 1994

used to log the timber around the shoreline. The logs were then towed to the railhead and loaded on railcars. Trucks were introduced in the 1940s and were used to haul logs from the sidehills and side valleys to the railway. In the early 1950s, tractor and arch yarding, in which logs were hauled from the woods behind tracked machinery, was introduced in areas such as Sutton Creek and Woss Lake.

In 1956 it became economically feasible to build a railway along the east side of Nimpkish Lake and do away with the booming, towing and reloading process. The system of trucks and railway is still in use today and represents the last logging railway in the province.

Doug Rickson retired in 1995 as chief forester of Canadian Forest Products Ltd. (Canfor), the company that holds the harvesting rights in the Nimpkish Valley. Rickson has been associated with logging in this area for thirty-one years. He reports that after over seventy years, the company has harvested less than half of the 137,000 hectares of

FREDERICK ARM, MAINLAND 1980

This area has been harvested by contract loggers for over twenty years, and with immediate reforestation by planting, supplemented with natural seeding, a vigorous second-growth stand has become established.

FREDERICK ARM, MAINLAND 1994

productive forest land in their Tree Farm Licence. In 1995, approximately 77,000 hectares remained in its natural old-growth state. Of the 60,000 hectares the company has harvested, over 95 percent now supports new forests.

"The forests that have regrown since logging in 1920s and 1930s are now about sixty to seventy years old," says Rickson. "They are beautiful stands. They have an average diameter of over 50 centimetres and I've seen spruce that are over 75 centimetres. It is impressive for the public to see a forest like this and realize that man didn't have a hand in reforesting it. Mother Nature did it and she did one hell of a job!"

Rickson says he has walked through the Nimpkish's sixty-year-old second-growth stands with many visitors. "They think they are in the forest primeval, until I start pointing out the old rotten stumps.

"It is easy for me to feel confident about the future of our second growth," Rickson continues. "I've been working in the woods for nearly forty years. I can recall driving up the Island Highway years ago and it was all clearcut on both sides and you had a grand view of the mountains. You drive through there now, but you can't see anything. You're going through a 'green tunnel' with trees 12 and 15 metres tall on either side. I guess that's where the general public don't have that advantage of seeing what actually happens over time. They see a bare clearcut and they compare that to the forest that was cut down and they don't see how that's going to come back. I've got no doubts in my mind at all—providing we keep the land base for commercial forestry—that the future is secure."

TOM BROWNE LAKE, MAINLAND 1977

Harvesting took place on this moderately steep slope with thin soil at Knight Inlet on the mainland coast. After logging, the area was slash burned and the rocky terrain was exposed. While mature trees never grew on the exposed rocks, pockets of soil were available between them to support new seedlings. As was the case here, planters select such pockets for the new stand. In the 1990s, a rocky slope such as this would probably not be slash burned, but immediately planted.

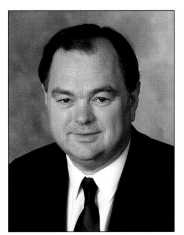

"There are more than 3,000 registered professional foresters in BC. The vast majority of us take our responsibility for care of the forests very seriously. In virtually every managed forest in the province, you will find dedicated people who are concerned and committed to ensuring that our forests are managed sustainably and managed properly."
Bill Dumont, *chief forester, Western Forest Products.*

TOM BROWNE LAKE, MAINLAND 1994

FOCUS ON CLEARCUTS

Not A Clear-cut Issue:
Mount Paxton and Changing Times

After appearing in a sensational full-colour spread in *National Geographic* magazine, the 140-hectare Mount Paxton logging site on northern Vancouver Island became a symbol in the case critics were building against British Columbia logging practices. The name became synonymous with huge, out-of-control clearcuts that were said to be turning fertile forest lands into permanent "moonscapes" over the length and breadth of the Pacific Northwest. Mount Paxton is still frequently evoked in the campaign to ban clearcutting.

Interestingly, Mount Paxton does not rank among the largest clearcuts in British Columbia, or even on Vancouver Island. At 140 hectares it would be dwarfed by a medium-sized burn like the 5,500-hectare Penticton wildfire of 1994. It is a modest knoll that even local people would have had a hard time putting a name to before *National Geographic* made it a household word. It was picked out for stardom because it stood off by itself in a conspicuous waterfront location and its steep slope had been logged from sea to sky.

At 140 hectares, the Mount Paxton clearcut would be dwarfed by a medium-sized forest fire like the 5,500-hectare Penticton fire of 1994. It was picked out for prominence because it stood off by itself in a conspicuous waterfront location and its steep slope had been freshly logged from sea to sky.

It made a strong, singular image—ideal for photographic purposes.

The company that logged Mount Paxton would be the first to admit it was done in an undesirable way. If they had a choice in the matter, logging would have proceeded quite differently. Fred Lowenberger, who was chief forester for International Forest Products Ltd. when Mount Paxton was logged, explains that plans in 1982 called for the eventual logging of all the timber on the hillside—but progressively, over an extended period, while leaving deferred patches of forest on several areas. At the time, provincial guidelines limited the size of clearcuts to 80 hectares annually.

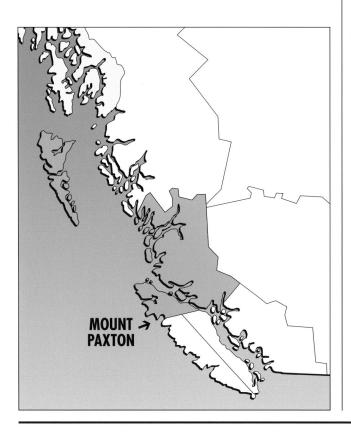

MOUNT PAXTON

Not A Clear-cut Issue

The lower face of the slope was logged first, over the course of three years. A 100-metre fringe of trees was left along the shoreline and a 150-metre strip on the rocky area near the ridge top.

Problems began in 1984, when the fringe of trees along the ocean blew down during one of the area's usual fall windstorms. The Forest Service then put up a timber sale to salvage the entire strip. More trouble came in the same year when a decision was made to burn the logging slash. "We got caught by a change of wind and the whole hillside caught fire and burned," says Lowenberger.

Although the trees were killed by the fire, they still had some commercial value, and to avoid total loss of the timber by leaving the dead trees to decay, a decision was made to initiate an immediate salvage operation. When that operation ended in 1989, the mountain looked much different than planned. The entire face was denuded, including the burned upper fringe. "When it was all logged," explains Lowenberger, "it became one large clearcut."

That is when the *National Geographic* photography crew came along and presented Mount Paxton to the world as a typical example of British Columbia forest practices.

But despite the fact that Mount Paxton unintentionally became a worst case scenario in forest practice terms, Lowenberger is able to report that ten years later the growing site is showing a strong recovery. "That hillside has its productive capacity intact, and 100 percent of it is growing back. We planted 1,000 Douglas fir, western red cedar and Sitka spruce seedlings per hectare, and when I was there in 1993 I noticed a lot of natural western hemlock regeneration coming in as well."

Lowenberger says the trees on the lower hillside, which were planted in the spring of 1986, are already over 6 metres tall. The trees on the top of the hillside, where the salvage logging was not completed until 1989, are understandably much smaller. "It is coming back to a vibrant young forest," he says. "It has lots of seedlings that are growing well with a good population of birds and wildlife."

Mount Paxton today stands as proof of the resilience of the coastal forest.

While the Mount Paxton clearcut became much larger than planned, openings of 100 hectares and more were common in British Columbia at the time. Until the mid-1980s, progressive clearcutting was the standard method of logging coastal valleys. Under this system, logging companies would take each year's allowance of timber progressively as they went up a valley. Each new clearcut would adjoin the last, with reforestation following a year or two after harvesting.

In 1972, the new Coast Harvesting Regulations limited the size of each cutblock, regardless of allowable annual cut, to 80 hectares. However, they could still be made progressively up a valley, with one year's cut adjoining the next.

Foresters had tried smaller clearcuts when accessing small pockets of valuable timber, but according to Fred Lowenberger, in areas where winter winds were severe, perimeter trees around the edges of these openings were often blown over. The larger the clearcut, the fewer edges there were to be blown down.

"Although entirely coincidental, those progressive clearcuts were similar to the way nature works," says Lowenberger. "Cutting large blocks of timber allows large blocks to be left, and this in turn promotes the maintenance of biological diversity."

In 1988, the Coastal Fish/Forestry Guidelines were introduced. They stipulated that mature patches of timber be left intact along streams, lakes and seashore. Progressive clearcutting was prohibited. In 1991, stricter regulations were introduced with the Interim Guidelines for Landscape Management and Recreation. These regulations introduced visual aesthetics as a forest resource value. Each clearcut now had to blend into the landscape to preserve visual values, most notably with viewscapes from highways and cruise ship routes.

"Over time, the visual effects of progressive harvesting became less and less desirable," explains Lowenberger. "More and more restrictions were placed on clearcutting as people placed more importance on protecting other values. The government reacted to those changes in public opinion by making changes in regulations."

In 1995, the Forest Practices Code limited the size of clearcuts to 40 hectares in the Vancouver, Kamloops and Nelson forest regions, and 60 hectares in the Prince Rupert, Cariboo and Prince George regions. While there is no doubt that small clearcuts are more appealing visually, there is continuing debate over the optimum size of clearcuts. Smaller clearcuts mean more wind damage and more roads—and roads cause more long-term damage to forest soils than any other factor. Many foresters hold that clearcuts should vary from small to large the way disturbances vary in nature, with the decision on clearcut size being determined by the local planning process which considers the Forest Practices Code and its relation to all forest uses. Harvesting practices throughout the province reflect a reduction in clearcut size.

Not A Clear-cut Issue

Original plans called for the eventual logging
of all the timber on this hillside—but
progressively, over an extended time period,
while leaving deferred patches of forest on
several areas. Problems began in 1984, when
the fringe of trees along the ocean blew down.
More trouble came when a slash fire got away
and burned the whole hillside. After the burned
timber was salvaged, it became
one large clearcut.

A black bear foraging on the logged slopes
of Mount Paxton in 1994.

Not A Clear-cut Issue

The lower slopes of Mount Paxton as viewed in 1994, showing how rapidly the plantation can convert a freshly logged area to a more pleasing panorama of second-growth saplings.

Following planting, the surfaces of the logging roads were broken up, recontoured, and seeded to grass to establish natural drainage flows.

Not A Clear-cut Issue

Fred Lowenberger (below), the forester in charge of logging Mount Paxton, stands next to 6-metre high trees planted in 1986 on the lower slopes of the mountain. In the photo (right), he stands by 2-metre high saplings planted in 1989 on the upper slopes. Throughout the clearcut, 1,000 Douglas fir, western red cedar and Sitka spruce seedlings were planted per hectare.

Not A Clear-cut Issue

In 1995, the Forest Practices Code limited the size of clearcuts in the Vancouver, Kamloops and Nelson forest regions to 40 hectares—less than one-third the size of the opening on Mount Paxton. Shown here are small clearcuts in the Greater Victoria watershed.

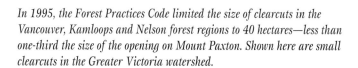

THE
FOREST
TOUR

Mist and Moss: The Forests of the West Coast of Vancouver Island

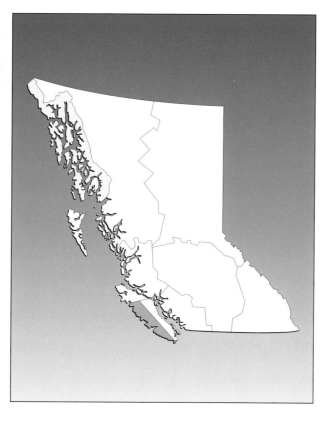

From far out in the open Pacific Ocean, huge rollers crash ashore on the reefs, rocky headlands and sweeping sandy beaches of the west coast of Vancouver Island. Gnarled, wind-bent shore pines and Sitka spruce line the headlands while western hemlock and balsam forests crowd up into the Island's mountain spine. In the lower reaches of those valleys are the ancient, towering stands of Sitka spruce and western red cedar which have become familiar to the world through campaigns to halt logging in the Carmanah and Walbran valleys. Cities and towns in this region that rely on the forest industry for a major portion of their income include Zeballos, Tahsis, Gold River and Ucluelet.

Fierce winter winds have kept the forests on exposed ridges fairly young, but the sheltered valleys of this region have been almost undisturbed by nature for close to 1,000 years. Succession has resulted principally from age and decay. Western red cedar may endure for a millennium, but balsam seldom live beyond 250 years and western hemlock 350. This has formed a multi-age forest.

For the first fifty or more years of harvesting, British Columbia's Douglas fir-hungry forest industry showed little interest in the forests of the west coast of Vancouver Island, which were primarily western hemlock and balsam. Railways from the east coast of the Island expanded across the divide in the 1920s, but interest in the west coast was limited to the scattered pockets of Douglas fir that grew in areas of lesser rainfall. When markets were good, Sitka spruce and western red cedar stands in the valley bottoms were also logged, but only the biggest and best trees were taken.

In 1906, one of the first railway operations accessing timber on the west coast began at Port Renfrew. Loggers targetted the prime stands of Douglas fir on the sheltered, leeward slopes of the San Juan Valley and Gordon River.

Early loggers on the west coast of Vancouver Island faced a major problem getting their wood to market. In order to reach the mills, logs had to be moved through waters subject to open ocean conditions. Attempts to use conventional flat booms led to crippling losses. In 1920, a new type of log boom was developed at Port Renfrew. The Davis raft was essentially a huge bundle of logs averaging 120 feet long and 70 feet wide, woven together with steel cables. These rafts were very expensive to construct, but they were sturdy and could withstand the big seas.

Although land access was easy, loggers were faced with the major problem of getting their logs to market. In order to reach mills on the shores of the Strait of Georgia, logs had to be moved through waters subject to open ocean conditions, and attempts to use conventional flat booms led to crippling losses. Various log transportation methods were tried but none was satisfactory until the development of the self-loading, self-dumping log barge in 1954.

With the area now accessible and markets opening up for western hemlock and balsam lumber and pulp, west coast logging expanded through the 1950s, aided by the development of portable yarding equipment and trucks suit-

ed to hauling in steep country. Still, harvesting operations progressed more slowly than elsewhere, and because of this, the area ended up having some untouched valley-bottom old-growth long after the great watershed forests had been logged in more accessible parts of the coast. Once logging roads afforded access to these remote areas and visitors were able to see the moss-covered giant Sitka spruce of the Walbran and Carmanah valleys for the first time, a powerful public lobby began to demand that they be protected from logging. International preservation campaigns made the Walbran, the Carmanah and Clayoquot Sound part of the world's environmental vocabulary and resulted in large areas of valley-bottom old-growth being preserved in parks

"THE BLACK HOLE" 1994

Nicknamed "The Black Hole," this slash-burned clearcut alongside the Port Alberni/Ucluelet highway achieved notoriety because of its ugly appearance. To Art Walker (above), the professional forester responsible for supervising reforestation, it was a "good burn," and the healthy regrowth in progress eight years later would seem to bear him out.

"Although clearcuts are never pretty, the combination of planted stock and natural reseeding have now resulted in a very successful plantation."
Art Walker, *forester.*

≺ *In the lower elevations of the sheltered, fog-shrouded valleys of the west coast of Vancouver Island, pockets of ancient, towering Sitka spruce, western red cedar and western hemlock remain. These areas have become familiar to the world through campaigns to halt logging in the Carmanah and Walbran valleys. This photo was taken in the Carmanah Valley.*

"THE BLACK HOLE" 1986 & 1994

"The resilience of the forest is really remarkable. There are very few harvested areas that I know of ... that are not well stocked with second-growth."
George von Westarp, *forester.*

Like "The Black Hole" (left and below), other cutblocks in the Ucluelet area (opposite) aroused public outcry when they were freshly harvested and burned. A decade later, healthy young stands of cedar and hemlock attract less attention.

UCLUELET 1971 & 1994

"Our experience with clearcutting has been a learning experience; we have learned some lessons and are still learning others."
Keith King, *forest research technician.*

or protected by other means. Logging that does take place adjacent to these areas is subject to extraordinary restriction.

MacMillan Bloedel Ltd. (MB), is the licensee of TFL #44 on the west coast of Vancouver Island. The coniferous forests of this TFL cover an area of 359,000 hectares. Of that, 206,739 hectares, or 57.5 percent, is in its natural old-growth state. A total of 152,000 hectares, or 42.5 percent of the total area, has been logged over the past 135 years. Ninety-eight percent of that area has returned to forest land. Only 2 percent of the area logged is currently not reforested.

George von Westarp has been a forester with MB for thirty-two years and is responsible for environmental audits of logging and silvicultural practices throughout the company's managed forest lands in coastal British Columbia. He has a thorough understanding of the state of MB's second-growth forests in this area.

Westarp says many areas of coastal British Columbia would regenerate well even if man didn't have a hand in restocking the harvested areas. The heavy carpet of forests that covered British Columbia when Europeans first arrived provide ample evidence that although the forests were repeatedly blown down, burned, or destroyed by insects and diseases, they always dominated in the end. "The resilience

CARNATION CREEK 1980

This area near Carnation Creek on Barkley Sound was logged in 1980 (right). In the photo below, forests have been restored to healthy levels fourteen years later.

CARNATION CREEK 1994

of the forest is really remarkable," he says. "There are very few harvested areas that I know of on MB lands that are not well stocked with second growth."

Westarp says it's usually difficult to tell if an area was planted or if it came back naturally, partly because of the mix of species that have "seeded in." "We plant about 60 percent of our areas now, with the remainder naturally seeded. Only 16 percent of our plantations have not had significant additional natural seed-in of other species. Those other species now make up at least 20 percent of our second-growth crop trees."

Westarp says that most of the planted areas that did remain in single species were in areas such as the dry Douglas fir zones where it has always grown as the dominant species.

"I'm very confident about the future of our second-growth forests. I think they are a fantastic resource that is generally healthier than the old growth. The majority of the areas that have been logged have quite uniform stocking of mainly conifers. They've been well planted—quality planted—which means the trees grow well and should remain healthy."

TOFINO FLATS 1975

This cutblock is behind Long Beach, outside of Pacific Rim National Park. After logging in 1975, the site was burned and planted. By 1994, the new forest was spaced to allow for better individual growth and portions were later pruned to obtain higher quality logs.

TOFINO FLATS 1994

TOFINO FLATS 1973

In this 1973 newspaper photo, forester Gerry Burch stands in a harvested and slash-burned cutblock. This area is close to Long Beach and was adjacent to the soon-to-be-created Pacific Rim National Park. (Below) Gerry Burch revisits the site in 1994, after twenty-one years.

TOFINO FLATS 1994

HILLCREST MID-1960s

HILLCREST 1994

Slash burning followed this clearcut on southern Vancouver Island. Regeneration is difficult on rocky knolls, as evidenced in this 1994 photo. Today, rocky slopes like this would be given greater consideration in planning harvesting.

HARRIS CREEK CAMP 1953

HARRIS CREEK CAMP 1994

This railroad logging camp (above) housed about 150 men at Harris Creek near Port Renfrew in 1953. The camp was closed in the early 1960s. The buildings were removed and the area planted. Very little evidence of the camp site remains today.

GORDON RIVER CAMP 1954

Harvesting took place throughout the Gordon River Valley near Port Renfrew for fifty years. In the centre of the photo (left) is the logging camp at Gordon River in 1954. By 1994, the valley had restocked very successfully through a combination of artificial and natural regeneration. The camp in the centre of the photo is still in operation.

GORDON RIVER CAMP 1994

NITINAT VALLEY 1969

NITINAT VALLEY 1994

This sizable 1969 clearcut in the Nitinat Valley (above) had regenerated successfully twenty-five years later. Nearby Nitinat Lake has become an internationally-renowned centre for sailboarding.

An eighty-year-old "plus tree" near Lake Cowichan. Plus trees are natural trees selected and tested for greater growth, better quality, superior wood characteristics and resistance to insects and disease. Once the trees are located, twigs are obtained from them and grafted onto root stocks in seed orchards. Initial trials were with Douglas fir, but soon spread to other species of native trees. By the year 2000, more than 50 percent of all seedlings planted in BC will be from seed obtained from these orchards. Many foresters believe that substantial gains in yield can be obtained from using genetics with native species. Among the pioneers in this field were professional foresters Dr. Alan Orr-Ewing and Dr. Oscar Sziklai with the co-operation of industrial foresters Gerry Burch, Sven Rasmussen, Bruce Devitt, Darryl MacQuillan and others.

In the 1960s Douglas fir was the only nursery stock produced by the Forest Service and it was planted extensively on the coast, but experience found that most areas which originally supported western hemlock or western red cedar should be planted to these species again. This deformed Douglas fir on the Tofino flats remains today as a reminder.

The Truth In Numbers: The State of the Vancouver Forest Region

The Lower Mainland, Vancouver Island, mid-Coast and the Queen Charlotte Islands together form the Vancouver Forest Region. In spite of the fact that the southern portion of the region has been logged longer and more intensively than any other part of British Columbia, the region still has 3.4 million hectares of mature timber, according to the 1993–94 Ministry of Forests Annual Report. This represents 63 percent of all productive forest land, including inaccessible areas, some parks as well as the working forest. Of the remainder, 1.8 million hectares, or 34 percent, is made up of immature forests (under 120 years old). Not-fully-stocked stands, mostly containing newly planted trees, non-commercial species, brush, and areas denuded by natural disturbances or harvesting, cover 133,000 hectares, or 2 percent of the area. In total, over 96 percent of the forest of the Vancouver Forest Region is growing forests of various ages (see Appendix).

Between 1984 and 1994, the average annual logging effort in the Vancouver Forest Region involved 38,486 hectares. This represents less than three-quarters of 1 percent of the productive forest land base, and compares to the ten-year average of 20,367 hectares of forest affected by natural causes such as wildfire, insects and diseases. Reforestation efforts saw the planting of over 21 million seedlings of 17 different species in 1994.

Nobody would deny the forest industry has left its mark on coastal British Columbia, but those who fear the province's land is being deforested cannot help but feel reassured by these facts.

Status of Productive Forest Land 1994

Vancouver Forest Region • Total 5.4 million hectares

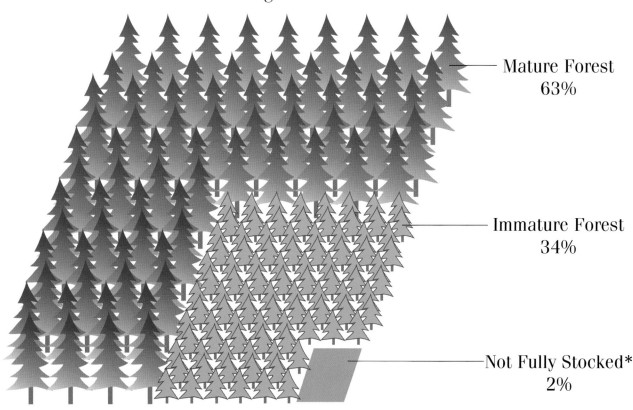

Mature Forest
63%

Immature Forest
34%

Not Fully Stocked*
2%

*includes areas denuded by fire and insects, stands of non-commercial trees and recent plantings.

Source: Ministry of Forests

Rivers and Streams: Fish Habitat and Logging

Many of British Columbia's rivers, streams and creeks provide extremely important habitat and spawning grounds for fish. Resident and sea-run trout and Dolly Varden char provide excellent sport fishing opportunities, and the six species of Pacific salmon that return to watercourses to spawn provide the bulk of British Columbia's commercial and sport fisheries. For many years there has been concern about damage to fish and fish habitat from timber harvesting activities.

Some of that concern was well-founded. For the first half of the century, the Forest Service and forest companies gave little thought to fish resources. In some instances, trees were felled into fish-bearing streams, logs were yarded across them and tractors driven through them. Siltation caused by logging clogged spawning gravel and suffocated eggs. Watercourses were left unprotected from sun for miles, raising water temperatures and disrupting natural migration timing. Uncontrolled runoff scoured away spawning gravel. Many fish populations were affected.

Jack Dryburgh was a divisional forester with MacMillan Bloedel on the west coast of Vancouver Island in the early 1970s. "The real value of leave strips along fish streams was not fully comprehended," he explains. "Today, we don't understand what foresters were going through back then. There was a lack of research. There was a lack of factual information. There was a lot of 'gut' feeling on the part of both fisheries and logging personnel, but there were no facts to back up any assumptions."

Carnation Creek on Vancouver Island's west coast (left)has been the site of over 150 scientific research papers examining the effects of logging on fish stocks. Findings have had a major effect on subsequent forest practices.

(Below) Rainbow trout.

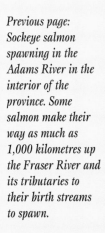

Previous page: Sockeye salmon spawning in the Adams River in the interior of the province. Some salmon make their way as much as 1,000 kilometres up the Fraser River and its tributaries to their birth streams to spawn.

That lack of knowledge was soon to change, and Dryburgh was to play an integral part.

In 1970, in order to understand the interaction among logging, fish and fish habitat—and to develop harvesting guidelines which would protect natural fisheries resources—a long-term study was initiated at Carnation Creek on Barkley Sound. This was a co-operative study by the British Columbia Forest Service, Ministry of the Environment, Federal Department of Fisheries and Oceans and the forest industry. MB held cutting rights in the area, and Dryburgh was the forester in charge. He was involved in those studies for a dozen years and says there were both positive and negative findings in even the worst-case scenario of logging through the creek (conducted for research purposes only). He notes that the study found there were certain situations where leave strips were of paramount importance and other situations, such as some small tributary creeks, where leave strips had substantially less value. "Each situation," he says, "needs to be evaluated on its own merits."

Over 150 scientific research papers were published as a result of the Carnation Creek studies, and the findings have played a major part in providing extensive information to government and forest companies so that timber harvesting activities can be carried out in a manner that is ecologically sound. The adoption of both the original Fish/Forestry Guidelines and the 1995 Forest Practices Code was based largely on the experience and research

*As with land animals, aquatic ones could never have
survived centuries of natural upheaval if they were
subject to extinction every time their habitat was dis-
rupted. What has been learned from watersheds like
Carnation Creek is that fish, like other forest creatures,
are capable of surviving short-term disruption.*

*(Photos this page)
Netting spawning salmon for
a forest-company hatchery on the Marble River.
The salmon are then flown in watertight baskets
to the hatchery where technicians
collect their eggs and milt.*

results from the Carnation Creek project.

In spite of efforts to mimic worst-case timber harvesting in several reaches, the trout continue to live in
Carnation Creek and the salmon continue to return. The
study, which is the longest running project of its kind in
North America, continued through 1995. Similar findings,
obtained from other creeks more severely affected by logging, showed fish populations could be re-established, and
sometimes came back stronger than before.

Dryburgh says he is confident that ongoing research
projects—working with wider leave strips and "feathering"
timber edges—will help ensure protection of fish and fish
habitat in sensitive areas.

From Railway Ties to Lumber: The Forests of the Interior

*T*he generally dry interior region of the province covers the broad expanse between the Coast and Rocky mountains. The region is dotted with lakes and characterized by cold, snowy winters and short, warm summers. In the northern reaches of the boreal and sub-boreal forest zones, only trees that can tolerate an extended period of frozen conditions are found.

The central portion of the interior is made up of a wide plateau of flatlands and rolling mountains. Farther south is an area of dry mountains and deep, semi-desert valleys. The ground cover in these areas is a mix of open grasslands and large expanses of forest.

Unlike the spectacular old growth in some regions of the coast, interior forests are generally much shorter lived—usually between 100 and 200 years. This is due in part to the genetic make-up of the species, which are adapted to continual natural disturbances such as wildfire and insects.

The first large-scale logging in the interior started over 100 years ago in order to supply timber for mining operations and ties and bridge timbers for the trans-continental railway lines. A single mile of track required thousands of ties. To meet the need, trees were felled by hand, hacked or sawn square and transported by horses and wagon to trackside. Flumes, river drives and log booms were also used to move trees to early sawmills, which also produced lumber for the settlements springing up adjacent to the railway. The railways provided a network of relatively inexpensive transportation and forest companies had ready access to markets. Once cleared, much of the fertile valley bottom land was used for agriculture and livestock production.

In the 1930s, log-hauling trucks were introduced which allowed loggers to extend their reach farther from processing mills and up steeper slopes. In the 1950s, war-surplus four-wheel-drive trucks began replacing horses in skidding logs from the woods. At the same time, cable yarding systems such as steel spars and grapple yarders were introduced to access the steepest terrain in some parts of the interior.

Logging operators, their transportation systems and the attendant infrastructure have made enormous contributions to the development of the province's interior and in the 1990s, 70 percent of British Columbia's forest products come from interior forests.

The construction of railways created an almost insatiable demand for rail ties. Over 3,000 ties were required for each mile of track.

≺ *A large, mature ponderosa pine in the Kootenays.*

Unmatched Diversity: The Forests of Southeastern British Columbia

Britsh Columbia's triangle-shaped Kootenays in the southeast corner of the province are the interior's most mountainous region. Mining first put the Kootenays on the map, as such towns like Nelson, Kaslo, New Denver, Kimberley and Trail were established. Ranching figured in the growth of Grand Forks and Cranbrook, but in the end lumbering became the region's leading industry.

Kootenay topography is characterized by three northwest-trending mountain ranges: the Monashees, Selkirks and Purcells, which lead eastward to the Rockies. The alternating high mountains and broad valley bottoms has created an environment which is host to the widest diversity of forest types in the province. The landscape ranges from ponderosa pine and bunchgrass in dry valley bottoms to glaciers and alpine tundra. Overall, three forest types dominate.

The highest-elevation tree-growing areas reach to the Subalpine and are characterized by shorter growing seasons,

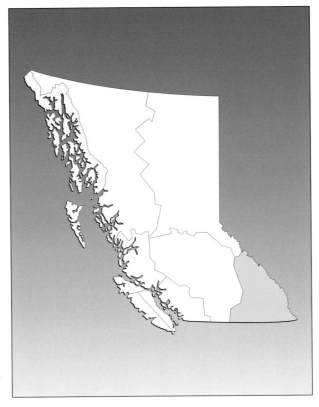

colder temperatures, and higher rainfall and snow than lower-elevation zones. They are dominated by Engelmann spruce and subalpine fir. The trees in this zone often live to 275 years.

In the lower- and mid-elevation areas of the eastern portion of the region—the Rocky Mountain Trench—the dominant species is interior Douglas fir, with a varying mix of western larch and lodgepole or ponderosa pines.

The wetter valley bottoms of the western portion of the region are home to Canada's only interior western red cedar–western hemlock forests. These interior trees are genetically different than their coastal counterparts in that they are shorter-lived, more susceptible to decay and have adapted to a much shorter growing season. Although this zone is subject to threats such as wildfire and insects, these stands can reach the age of 350 years and some specimens have reached diameters of 2 metres.

For thousands of years wildfire has served as a force of renewal in the forests of British Columbia's interior region. Shown here is an edge of the 1994 Lumberton fire which threatened houses and settlements and resulted in the evacuation of 300 people.

The Dewar Creek Valley is part of the Purcell Wilderness Conservancy in the Kootenays. These high-elevation old-growth forests are a combination of Engelmann spruce and subalpine fir.

(Below) Bag booms are used to transport logs on Slocan Lake.

Forester John Murray.

Over much of the area, natural disturbances play a major role in the life of the forest. Each year, tens of thousands of hectares of forest are destroyed by insects. In 1992, for example, 186,000 hectares were infested by a single pest, the western hemlock looper, and up to 80 percent of the affected trees died. In the days before modern fire-fighting, those trees would have dried out and fallen, creating fuel for an inevitable lightning strike and wildfire—fires that sometimes burned valley after valley from river bottom to treeline. As it was historically, wildfire remains a major natural disturbance to Kootenay forests. Over 60,000 hectares were consumed in seven major forest fires during the dry summer of 1985.

Despite almost 100 years of logging and a history of wildfire and insect infestations, in 1994 only 5 percent of the region's productive forest land was not forested—and most of that was in the process of recovering from recent natural disturbances.

Dave Basaraba has worked as a forester with Crestbrook Forest Industries Ltd. in the east Kootenays for nineteen years. He claims that the biggest problem facing the forests of the region is too much natural regeneration. "Nature has done an amazing job of bringing the forests

LUSSIER RIVER 1978

This site was logged in 1978 and then drag scarified. This site preparation method involves dragging heavy chains or barrels behind a tractor to expose the soil so that seeds will germinate more efficiently. This site was spaced in 1993.

LUSSIER RIVER 1994

back. If regeneration was a problem, there wouldn't be any trees growing on these hillsides. In fact, we can't hold back nature. Some people are saying there is no grass left to browse out there—that there are too many trees!"

Basaraba believes that man has much less of an impact on the forests than nature. "People say that after clearcutting it is all destroyed, but clearcutting has less of an impact than Mother Nature's wildfires, because we can control the amount of clearcutting done."

Jack Raven began working as a forest ranger in the Kootenays in 1947. He retired from the Forest Service in 1981 after thirty-four years in the woods. Raven has two sons, both foresters, who now carry on the family tradition. "I have no worries about the ability of the forests to keep growing trees," says Raven. "There were trees growing back then and who knows how many rotations or how many different forests have been on any area."

Like Basaraba, Raven is confident that timber harvesting has not adversely affected the environment. "I don't know of an area that didn't come back after logging. Some of it you can't even walk through. Our problem in the interior hemlock–cedar zone is not regeneration, it's overstocking."

LUSSIER RIVER 1978

A cutblock near the lower Lussier River in 1978. Larch trees were left on site to aid in natural regeneration. The new forest grew back to a mixture of pine and larch. The new growth came in so densely that to avoid stagnation the stand was spaced to 1,200 stems per hectare in 1993.

LUSSIER RIVER 1994

"Nature has done an amazing job of bringing the forests back. If regeneration was a problem, there wouldn't be any trees growing on these hillsides. In fact, we can't hold back nature. Some people are saying there is no grass left to browse out there—that there are too many trees!"
Dave Basaraba, forester.

Jack Raven was a ranger with the BC Forest Service for forty years. In the 1950s, he was interested in restocking a very large timber sale in the Nakusp area. There was no source of seedlings at that time, so he drove along the road, collecting seedlings as he went, and then planted them in a harvested area. In 1994, he revisited his plantation. Said Raven: "I have no worries about the ability of the forests to keep growing trees. There were trees growing back then and who knows how many rotations or how many different forests have been on any area."

The Truth In Numbers: The State of the Forests of Southeastern BC

The forests of southeastern British Columbia, form the area known as the Nelson Forest Region. The productive forests of this area cover 3.3 million hectares. Forty-one percent (1.4 million hectares) is covered in mature forests. Of the remainder, 53 percent (1.8 million hectares) is made up of immature forests. The large amount of immature forests—the highest percentage of any forest region in the province—is mostly the result of very dry summers and massive forest fires that took place in the early part of the century. In the 1990s, the resultant new forests are still classed as immature and only 5 percent of the productive forest (183,000 hectares) is considered not-fully-stocked. In total, 94.5 percent of the productive forest land of the Nelson Forest Region is growing forests of various ages (see Appendix).

Between 1984 and 1994, the average annual timber harvesting effort in the Kootenay area involved 26,527 hectares. This represents less than 1 percent of the productive forest and compares with the ten-year average of 52,147 hectares affected by wildfires and insect infestation. In 1994, reforestation efforts saw the planting of over 17 million seedlings of twelve different species. Although most of the working forest of the Kootenays is classified as immature, the important fact is that 95 percent of the productive forest land is still growing trees.

Status of Productive Forest Land 1994

Nelson Forest Region • Total 3.3 million hectares

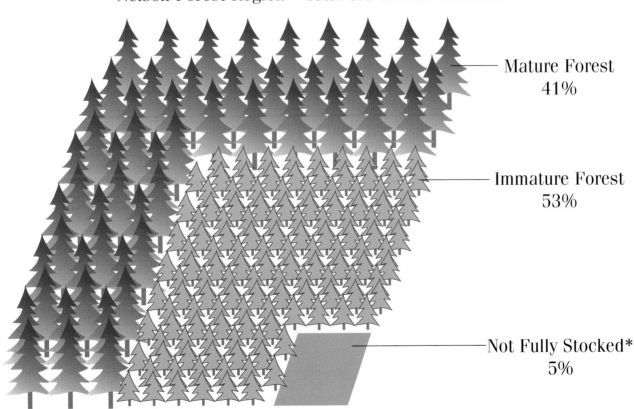

Mature Forest
41%

Immature Forest
53%

Not Fully Stocked*
5%

*includes areas denuded by fire and insects, stands of non-commercial trees and recent plantings.

Source: Ministry of Forests

The Saint Mary's Lake area north of Cranbrook. Largely due to salvaging timber destroyed by the mountain pine beetle, extensive logging incorporating large clearcuts took place in this drainage in the early 1970s. Portions were drag scarified after logging. Machine planting was used in a few areas. Generally, though, the area was naturally regenerated. Many of the new stands were spaced in 1993, at twenty years of age.

(Below) In this mature stand, the larch trees are beginning to yellow. Larch is a unique conifer in that, like deciduous species, it sheds its needles in winter.

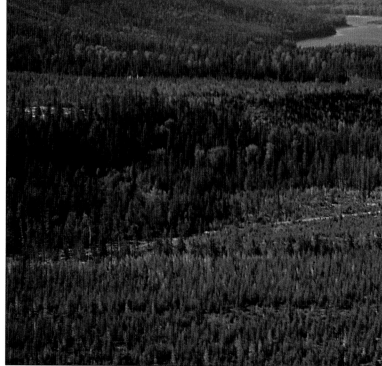

"For my father, my brother and me, forestry is much more than a career or profession. It has become our reason for being, and together we have close to one hundred years of experience. Having watched forests change, both naturally and after logging, we continue to marvel at the beauty and complexity of forest ecosystems."
David Raven, *forester.*

This cutblock was machine planted. Machine planting is sometimes used after logging has taken place on flat ground with a good gravel base.

All Creatures Great and Small: Wildlife And Logging

British Columbia continues to be blessed with an abundance and rich variety of wildlife after over a century of logging. The province today is home to 110 species of land-based mammals, nearly 80 percent of the Canadian total according to the 1994 BC Forest, Range and Recreation Resource Analysis. The province also supports more large (greater than 1 kilogram) mammal species than any other province or state in North America, including deer, elk, moose, caribou, mountain sheep, mountain goat, gray wolf, cougar, grizzly bear, black bear and wolverine.

In nature, animal populations are always in a state of flux, increasing and decreasing with food availability, habitat, and predator–prey relationships. Natural disturbances like wildfire have traditionally had the greatest effect on wildlife. With the onset of fire, for example, animals usually survive but may need to move to an unburned area. When new growth begins in a burn, populations of browsing animals like bear, moose, deer and grouse have more food and as a result generally increase in numbers. This in turn provides more food for predators like cougar and wolves and those populations increase proportionally. As the forest canopy closes overhead, the amount of browse decreases and animal populations move on, die of hunger or become prey. As the forest matures, it continues to support fewer and fewer large mammals. Most large animals that use the mature forests do so primarily for protection from predators, or for food like lichen when the snow cover is too deep for foraging in open areas.

In nature, animal populations are always in a state of flux, increasing and decreasing with food availability, habitat, and predator–prey relationships.

(Left) A large Rocky Mountain bull elk browses in a clearcut.

A young boar grizzly bear on British Columbia's north coast.

An osprey returns
to its nest atop log
boom pilings on
Ootsa Lake.

A white-tailed deer
browses in a clearing.

A bald eagle feeds on the carcass of a
spawned-out salmon.

With the reduction in area burned by wildfires from 220,000 hectares per year seventy years ago to an average of 55,000 hectares in the 1990s, the total area of natural forage created by wildfire has been reduced. In fact, between 1989 and 1993, an average of over 45,000 hectares of shrub, forest and grassland per year were intentionally burned to enhance forage for wildlife and cattle.

Similar to wildfire, clearcut timber harvesting creates clearings that provide important forage for large mammals.

Today, wildlife is one of the most important considerations when planning timber harvests. Wildlife resources must be assessed and, before any harvesting is allowed in an area, foresters must assure government agencies that logging will not infringe upon important wildlife habitat. Where wildlife could be adversely affected, reserves of standing timber are left intact. These reserves may include critical winter range, wildlife corridors, high feeding areas and breeding and rearing areas. For the larger birds, nesting sites are left intact, and for small birds like woodpeckers, snags (dead trees) and potential snags are sometimes left or erected to provide habitat after logging.

One of the primary ways to maintain wildlife popula-

Today, managing for wildlife is one of the most important considerations when planning timber harvests. Wildlife resources must be assessed and before any harvesting is allowed in an area, foresters must assure government agencies that logging will not infringe upon important wildlife habitat. For large birds, nesting sites are left intact and for small birds like woodpeckers, snags (dead trees) are sometimes left or erected to provide habitat after logging.

tions is to ensure that a variety of habitats is always available.

Jim Burbee, chief forester for Prince George-based Northwood Pulp and Timber Ltd., explains: "There are species of wildlife that prefer old forests, other species that prefer young forests and some species that prefer clearcuts. You'll find those animals where those things occur. The trick," he says, "is to keep some of each around." He notes that in the past, this was accomplished not by design, but as a result of British Columbia's sustained yield policy. "You had to measure your cut to make it last sustainably and by doing this you levelled out the distribution of age classes so some of each type of habitat was around."

Trevor Jeanes is a forester who has extensive practical experience in the relationship between logging and wildlife populations in the central part of the province. In areas where the dense pine stands of the southern interior have been thinned, says Jeanes, ungulate (hoofed mammal) production often increases tenfold. "We can produce deer like you wouldn't believe in this area. We've demonstrated it and the wildlife biologists agree.

"We've got areas of our forest that were so thick with windfall and debris that no animal could get through there.

(Above left) One of the primary ways to maintain wildlife populations is to ensure that a variety of habitats is maintained.

(Above right) Roosevelt elk herds are predominant within the working forests of central and northern Vancouver Island.

(Left) A moose in a swampy portion of the Bowron Lakes.

After it was clearcut, the moose and the deer moved into the area and productivity is incredible. They weren't even there before. From the point of view of wildlife as we know it, harvesting of trees has been a very beneficial thing."

At the same time Jeanes points out that there are other animals that don't benefit from opening the forest. "There are forms of wildlife such as rare birds that need the old-growth canopy to survive. We haven't destroyed that habitat."

Jack Raven agrees that some animals benefit from logging: "As soon as you log, you get fresh young brush and berries and young conifer buds that attract the deer and elk, and all of the little animals benefit from logging. If there are caribou in the country, in the morning they are right where you're logging because they eat the lichen off the felled trees.

"We don't log whole valleys. We haven't for years and there are always unlogged areas for the animals to go to. If they want to eat, they come into the logged area."

Forester Dick Kosick says deer populations on Vancouver Island are much higher now than ever before and are increasing more and more each year. "I don't think there has been a negative impact from logging on the wildlife. If anything the deer population has become a problem to some plantations."

Some species never enter the deep forest; others never leave it. Still others, like the marbled murrelet, enter it only for special purposes. Different animals require different things of the forest. What is required to satisfy the full spectrum of British Columbia wildlife is a multi-textured forest with a mix of open areas and canopied areas. As natural disturbance like fire becomes less prevalent, logging can play a beneficial role in maintaining the necessary diversity.

THE FOREST TOUR

Renewal by Fire: The Forests of the Central and Southern Interior

The central and southern interior regions of British Columbia comprise the vast area between the Rocky Mountains, the Kootenays and the Coast Mountains. The most notable geographic features of the area are the broad Cariboo uplands plateau of the central interior and the dry, rolling mountains of the southern interior. Towns with significant dependence on the forest industry are Princeton, Ashcroft, Merritt, 100 Mile House, Golden, Revelstoke, Williams Lake, Quesnel and the McBride–Valemount and North Thompson areas.

Rainfall here is sparse—averaging less than 40 centimetres per year—and the region is subject to dry, hot summers and cold winters.

The forests of the southern interior region are made up of ponderosa pine and bunchgrass in the drier, lower-elevation areas; western red cedar and western hemlock in the wetbelt areas; interior Douglas fir and lodgepole pine on the mid-elevation mountainsides; and Engelmann spruce and subalpine fir to the alpine.

The forests of the central interior on the dry, interior

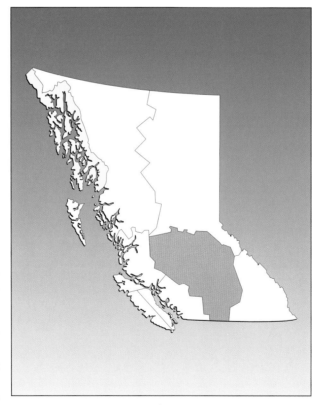

plateau support the largest unbroken tracts of lodgepole pine in the province. This relatively short-lived species has adapted to a unique set of environmental conditions, most notably regular insect infestations and wildfire. Lodgepole pine is considered to be mature at 80 years and seldom lives longer than 250 years. As these even-aged stands pass maturity and begin to decay, they lose their natural ability to fend off insects. Those insects—most notably bark beetles—seek out stands of old and weakened trees and set up housekeeping. Their numbers soon multiply exponentially as they attack the remaining vigorous trees and eradicate the entire stand. In 1984, at the height of the most recent epidemic, almost 500,000 hectares of lodgepole pine forest in the interior were infested with the mountain pine beetle.

As individual trees die, they either topple or are blown over by wind. The trees dry out quickly on the ground. Historically, fire followed. A single lightning storm has been known to produce 10,000 lightning strikes and start more

Old-growth lodgepole pine stands north of Kamloops. The forests of the central interior on the dry, interior plateau support the largest unbroken tracts of lodgepole pine in the province. Lodgepole pine is considered to be mature at 80 years and seldom lives longer than 250 years.

The brown-hued spruce trees in this photo (above) are being attacked by spruce bark beetles. The younger age of forests in the interior is due in part to the genetic make-up of the species, which are adapted to continual natural disturbances. (Right) Natural blowdown, or wind-falls, happen regularly in the forests of British Columbia. As shown here, blowdown often occurs in mature stands. If possible, such areas are harvested immediately, both to recover the value of the logs before they rot and to remove a potential breeding site for bark beetles.

than 300 blazes. Sometimes the fires were limited to small patches, others burned vast areas.

Lodgepole pine—like coastal Douglas fir—has adapted to wildfire and usually regenerates most prolifically following a fire because, the cones open, seeds are released and the new seedlings are exposed to full sunlight. While the cones from most tree species are consumed by fire, a large number of lodgepole pine seeds are protected by a unique resinous seal on the cones which breaks down in the heat of the fire. As the fire burns itself out, the seeds fall out of the cone and begin to regenerate in the exposed soil. Regeneration is usually quick and abundant with up to 400,000 seedlings per hectare becoming established. As the new lodgepole pine forest grows, each seedling must fight for its share of sunlight, moisture and nutrients. Unlike most coastal forests, where stands thin themselves naturally, lodgepole pine stands can become so thick that there is not enough moisture to go around, and the stands stagnate.

There is no doubt that man has had an effect on the natural cycle of insects and wildfire in the interior. Beetle populations were historically balanced by natural fires, but modern fire-fighting technology has greatly increased the forester's ability to control wildfire. As a result, there are more older forests and beetle populations have skyrocketed. To minimize the insect problem, forest companies must often focus part of their annual harvest on salvaging insect-killed or infested trees before they become unmerchantable or are destroyed by wildfire. In areas already burned by fire, timber is salvaged before it dries out and loses its value.

Control of fires has also resulted in increasing accumulations of dry fuels on the forest floor, which makes a blaze harder to stop when it does occur. This was evident during the 5,500 hectare Penticton fire of 1994, which burned out of control for days, destroying both forests and homes.

Some interior tree species have adapted to fire as a stimulus to regeneration. The seeds of lodgepole pine are protected from being burned by a unique resinous seal on the cones which breaks down in the heat of the fire. As the wildfire burns itself out, the seeds fall out of the cone and begin to regenerate in the exposed soil.

Randy Chan is the manager of environment and forestry for Tolko Industries Ltd., one of the larger forest companies in the central interior. Chan has worked as a forester in the area for twenty-four years. He says that of the 1.5 million cubic metres his company harvests each year, recently over 50 percent has been concentrated on stands attacked by the bark beetles. "When you plan your logging," explains Chan, "you obviously address the damaged trees but you also look at the older stands adjacent to current infestations which are highly susceptible to attacks. You try to leave the younger stands that are more vigorous to continue to grow."

Chan notes that the technology to harvest and manufacture small-diameter lodgepole pine economically was not perfected until the mid-1960s. As a result, vast areas of mature and overmature lodgepole pine, which are extremely susceptible to bark beetle attack, exist on large portions of the interior plateau. Chan speculates that in the past, universal fires may have occurred, resulting in the vast areas of even-aged stands found today. With these stands having matured, and with man having harvested only a small fraction of these stands, the recent peak in beetle populations may be nature's way of starting the cycle of renewal of the central interior's pine forests.

COMMUNITY LAKE 1974

This site in the Community Lake area near Kamloops was logged in 1974. The sign explains that 16,000 lodgepole pine seedlings were planted over 53 acres. The new forests shown on this and the opposite page are managed for both timber and range. In the early stages of these new forests, browsing cattle helped keep willows and trembling aspen brush from overtaking the new seedlings.

COMMUNITY LAKE 1994

As harvesting operations "chase" the beetle outbreaks, foresters like Chan say the new forests that regenerate are managed so that they will not get so dense they become stagnant. Traditionally, harvested areas were allowed to regenerate naturally. Areas where there was an abundance of lodgepole pine cones prior to logging, came back well, while areas where there were few cones tended to regenerate sparsely.

Chan explains that drag scarifying is often used as an alternative to slash burning after harvesting lodgepole pine. To expose the soil and allow the area to regenerate naturally, heavy chains or barrels are dragged over the ground. Not

Forester Randy Chan speculates that in the past, universal fires may have occurred, resulting in the vast areas of even-aged forests found today. Now that these stands are once again mature, and with man having only harvested a small fraction of them, the recent peak in beetle populations may be nature's way of starting the cycle of renewal of the central interior's pine forests.

DEVICK LAKE 1974

The new forest in the photo below is discoloured due to an infestation of needle blight, a non-fatal disease.

DEVICK LAKE 1994

FALKLAND 1952

every pine cone needs fire to release its seed; encouraged by the heat of summer and the increased radiation from the exposed soil, many cones still open and release their seeds. Planting is generally not required on lodgepole pine sites, but can help speed up and evenly distribute the regeneration.

To avoid difficulties in overstocking, stands are generally spaced as required. The optimum spacing for pine is 1,000 to 1,200 stems per hectare. This may involve manually plucking excess seedlings from the ground, cutting them out with garden shears, or using chain saws.

"We're really just trying to emulate Mother Nature," Chan explains. "If we're doing anything at all, we're just maybe speeding up the process. The forests are coming back very well."

Forester Trevor Jeanes agrees: "Man is kidding himself if he thinks he is managing the forests. Nature manages it. All man can do is assist nature."

The role of selection logging—partial cutting as opposed to clearcutting in interior forests—has been controversial. Some say it should be used more often while others insist it is used too much. There is no doubt, however, that partial cutting is much more aesthetically pleasing than clearcutting.

Partial cutting is not new to the forests of British

Columbia. When loggers first began harvesting the forests of the interior in the early 1900s, felling trees with axes and saws was a laborious process.

Most of British Columbia's partial cutting now takes place on gentle terrain in stands of ponderosa pine and interior Douglas fir, which are often mixed with western larch, spruces or pines. Most of these forests are found in the southern interior. Foresters try to regulate the size and species that are removed to maintain the genetic strengths of a stand. With trees removed from a stand, the new spacing allows more moisture and sunlight to reach the soil.

There are several reasons why interior Douglas fir and ponderosa pine are suited to selection systems. A deep taproot makes the species more windfirm than other species, therefore less likely to blow down when surrounding trees are removed from the stand. In addition, while coastal Douglas fir is not shade tolerant, the interior variety is partially shade tolerant and will regenerate somewhat in the shade of the larger trees. Like the process of thinning, "opening" the stand allows more moisture to fall through the canopy to the soil.

Although interior Douglas fir and ponderosa pine are the species best suited to selection systems, there are many factors that limit its use. It can only be used on dry sites where machinery will not unduly compact the soil, and it

FALKLAND 1994

(Opposite page) This area north of Falkland was harvested in 1952. Prior to the construction of pulp mills in the interior of the province, only high-grade sawlogs were removed from a logged stand. Lesser-quality logs were left on the ground.

(Above) The same site naturally regenerated with a mix of pine and spruce.

(Right) The same forest viewed from the ground.

can only be used on gentle terrain so that felled trees will not roll downslope when being yarded from the woods and scar the standing timber or crush the young trees.

Another limiting factor to partial cutting in Douglas fir is insects. The spruce budworm, despite its name, preys on Douglas fir. It likes to fall from the upper canopy onto young trees below, which in some areas has negated benefits of the selection approach.

Root rot is also proving to be a problem in some Douglas fir stands. The only proven way to rid the stand of root rot is to clearcut it and encourage a resistant species to occupy the site for forty years or so until the rot dies out.

Partial cutting has been tried in stands where lodgepole pine and spruces dominate. These stands make up a major portion of the forests of the central interior. Yet lodgepole pine and the spruces have shallow, lateral root systems which do not stand up to the increased exposure to wind after the forest canopy is opened.

In 1994, partial cutting accounted for less than 15 percent of the area harvested on Crown lands in British Columbia—largely because the system is only suited to a very specialized set of species, age classes and terrain. Where ecologically appropriate, however, it is becoming more widely used.

As the trees in second-growth stands reach merchantable size, commercial thinning operations will become commonplace to remove the dead, dying or diseased trees, to space the stands for increased growth, and to salvage mortality.

KELOWNA 1987

This area was part of a 4,000 hectare mountain pine beetle infestation. This block was harvested, site prepared and naturally regenerated. To minimize the problem of insect infestations, forest companies often focus part of their annual harvest on salvaging insect-killed or infested trees before they become unmerchantable or are destroyed by wildfire. In areas already burned by fire, harvesting operations are also focussed on salvaging the timber before it dries out and becomes valueless to industry.

KELOWNA 1994

A 120-year-old stand of unmanaged Douglas fir in the interior dry belt (left). The stand pictured lower left was partially cut in 1943, 1974 and 1981. Some pruning was undertaken to produce clear wood. Dry belt Douglas fir is one of the forest types in the province most suited to selection harvesting systems. In 1994, partial cutting accounted for approximately 15 percent of the area harvested on Crown lands in British Columbia.

Forester Trevor Jeanes (lower right) displays two Douglas fir rounds from trees growing 100 yards apart. The smaller one on the left is 120 years old and came from the unmanaged stand pictured above. The log on the right is twenty-two years old and came from the selection harvested stand. This shows how yields can be increased through intensive forest management.

120 Years Old

22 Years Old

The Truth In Numbers: The State of the Forests of the Southern and Central Interior

The southern and central interior areas of British Columbia make up the Kamloops and Cariboo Forest Regions. The productive forests of these regions comprise 10.4 million hectares. Fifty-nine percent (6.1 million hectares) is covered in mature forests. Of the remainder, 35 percent (3.7 million hectares) is made up of immature forests. Six percent of the area is classified as not fully stocked. In total, 94 percent of the productive forest of the central and southern interior is growing forests of various ages (see Appendix).

Between 1984 and 1994, the average annual harvest-ing effort involved 76,803 hectares. This represents three-quarters of 1 percent of the productive forest and compares to the average of 114,946 hectares of forest affected by natural causes such as wildfires and insect infestation over the same period.

Reforestation efforts saw the planting of over 59 million seedlings of eight different species in 1994. With 94 percent of the land base growing trees, the working forest of the central and southern interior is in no danger of disappearing.

Status of Productive Forest Land 1994

Kamloops and Cariboo Forest Regions • Total 10.4 million hectares

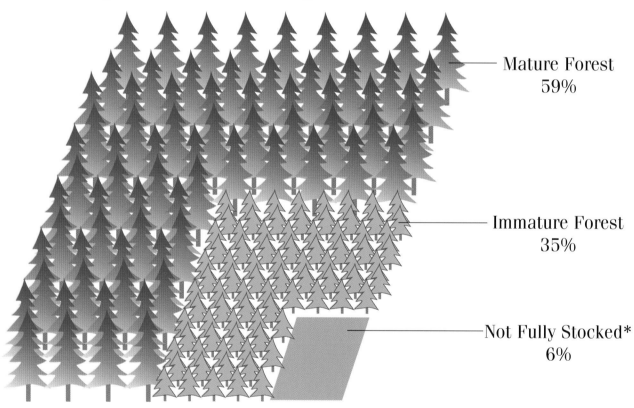

Mature Forest
59%

Immature Forest
35%

Not Fully Stocked*
6%

*includes areas denuded by fire and insects, stands of non-commercial trees and recent plantings.

Source: Ministry of Forests

Free Access:
Recreation in the Working Forest

British Columbia is a land of such natural splendour only the most jaded could remain indifferent to its outdoor attractions. The recreational opportunities offered by its bountiful natural environment draw millions of visitors and are always listed by residents as one of their chief sources of enjoyment.

Because 56 percent of British Columbia's lands are not serviced by roads, access remains a crucial factor in the distribution of recreational activities. This has made the forest industry one of the most important contributors to recreation. The vast majority of roads that do give access to wilderness areas were constructed to access Crown timber in provincial forests and fully two-thirds of all outdoor recreation occurs in areas accessible by forest roads. In 1992 it was estimated that only 16 percent of British Columbia's adult population undertook wilderness recreation trips to a roadless, undeveloped natural area accessible only by trails, waterways or air.

British Columbians place great importance on the recreation resources on public forest lands. Recent studies show that half the population uses Forest Service campsites and that the average resident spends 15 days per year participating in outdoor recreation in provincial forests. The

Forest Service has estimated that 88 million visitor days of outdoor recreation were made on public lands in British Columbia in 1993. Over half (55 million) of those visits took place in provincial forests. The balance was made up of visits to regional, provincial and national parks.

Provincial forests have always been open to the public but historically they were managed from an industrial point of view—for logging and mining. As the population of British Columbia grew and the forest industry opened up access to the forests through the construction of forest roads, people were able to spend more of their leisure time in the forests. The government was soon made aware of the importance of the forest not only for recreation, but also for its social, spiritual and environmental values.

In 1978, new legislation established recreation as one of the three primary resource management mandates of the Forest Service. Amendments to the Forest Act recognized wilderness as a distinct resource and legitimate land use in 1987. The Forest Service was mandated to provide increased opportunities for both residents and visitors to participate in a wide range of recreation activities in provincial forests.

Today the Forest Service oversees more than 3,150 managed and unmanaged recreation sites ranging from a

Back-country horse-packing in the Cariboo.

Because of British Columbia's multiple use policy, public forest lands are kept open to recreational use. Thanks to roads, campsites and other improvements made by the forest industry and Forest Service, the working forest is one of the province's most popular recreational resources.

(Above left) Pocket wilderness adjacent to the Marble River in the working forest of Vancouver Island.

(Above right) This low-key campsite in second growth near the Marble River is one of many that forest companies and the Forest Service maintain for the public in the working forest.

(Left) Forest companies also set aside special pockets of notable old growth for the public to enjoy.

few hectares to over 5,000 hectares in a variety of settings in both old and new forests.

British Columbia Forest Service campsites are generally rustic and simple, with no running water or electricity. They usually accommodate about ten vehicles and are designed to blend with their natural setting and offer basic sanitary facilities, fire rings, picnic tables and, where appropriate, boat launching ramps. No user fees are collected.

In addition, provincial forests offer more than 5,000 kilometres of managed recreation trails, ranging in length from a few kilometres to several hundred kilometres. These include summer hiking and horseback trails and winter trails for activities such as cross-country skiing and snowmobiling. There are also thousands of kilometres of trails in provincial forests not actively managed by the Forest Service. These trails range from natural wildlife trails to trails developed and maintained by recreation groups or commercial recreation users such as guide-outfitters.

There are also approximately 16,000 kilometres of rivers navigable by canoe, kayak or raft that flow through lands under the jurisdiction of the Forest Service.

British Columbians have a tradition of expecting free access to public forest lands, whether in logged or natural areas, and most outdoor recreation activities take place in

British Columbians have a tradition of expecting free access to public forest lands, whether in logged or natural areas, and the bulk of all forest recreational activities takes place in the working forest. According to a Ministry of Forests survey, over 96 percent of British Columbians find it either acceptable or desirable to locate their recreational activities in areas that have been logged but are now growing new stands of trees. Recreation opportunities enjoyed by British Columbians and visitors include fishing (Chilcotin), cross-country skiing (Monashee Mountains), wilderness fly-in camping (Clayoquot Sound) and four-wheel exploring (Lower Mainland).

forest that has been logged. According to the Ministry of Forests' 1989/90 Outdoor Recreation Study, over 96 percent of British Columbians find it acceptable or desirable to enjoy recreation in areas that have been logged but are now growing new stands of trees. In addition, almost two-thirds of those who use provincial forests find it acceptable or desirable for those activities to take place in areas where modification or change, such as logging, are evident and not yet completely revegetated. Ninety percent of those who use Forest Service recreation sites say they are satisfied with the experience and that their expectations were met.

Logging is often thought of as being incompatible with recreational use of the forest, but this is largely because opponents of logging focus on the small percentage of the working forest which is actively being logged or has recently been logged. As the statistics show, the government's multiple use strategy has been successful in accommodating recreational interests in the larger part of the working forest which supports old growth or maturing regrowth. In this light, the forest industry may be seen as a major benefactor of recreation. Not only does it provide important improvements such as roads, it is largely responsible for maintaining some 20 million hectares of working forest which is kept open to recreational use.

Almost Endless:
The Forests of the Northern Interior

Three hundred kilometres of flatlands and rolling hills—known as the interior plateau—span the width of British Columbia's northern interior region. Important cities with significant forest industry dependence are Prince George, Vanderhoof, Fort St. James, Mackenzie, Chetwynd, Dawson Creek, and Fort Nelson.

To the west and east, the foothills of the Coast and Rocky mountains rise up into rugged snow-capped peaks. To the south lie the extensive lodgepole pine forests of the central interior, and Canada's great boreal forest sweeps up into the far north. Winters are cold, snowy and long, while summers are warm, dry and short—with an average frost-free period of only three months. Precipitation is generally sparse, averaging 45 centimetres per year—most in the form of snowfall.

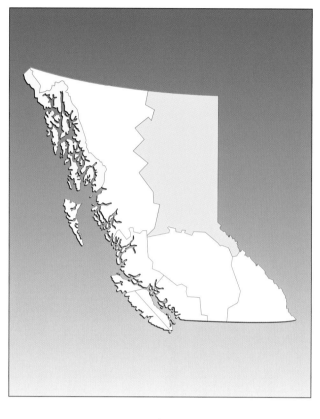

The sub-boreal forests of the northern interior are a diverse mix of coniferous and deciduous forests. The abundance and variety of species within this region, as elsewhere, is dependent on soils, nutrients and climate. White/ Engelmann spruce (a natural hybrid), sub-alpine fir and lodgepole pine are the dominant coniferous species. The deciduous species found in both pure and mixed stands include trembling aspen, paper birch and black cottonwood.

As with the changes in species by soil and climate, nature's renewal of the sub-boreal forests also changes accordingly. If free from wildfire and insect infestation, some spruce and true fir stands can live for up to 350 years—very old by interior standards. However, natural succession has historically resulted from fire. Even with today's fire-fighting advances, hundreds of wildfires annually consume 33,069 hectares in the northern interior, over half of the provincial total.

In the 1980s, one of the most severe outbreaks of insects on record—in this case the spruce bark beetle—occurred in the Bowron River watershed, an area prized for its wilderness values. The outbreak, which was soon epidemic, led to a salvage operation on over 50,000 hectares and the creation of the largest and most controversial man-made clearcut in British Columbia history.

*Young white spruce trees
in the northern interior.*

Three hundred kilometres of flatlands and rolling hills—known as the interior plateau—span the width of British Columbia's northern interior region.

The forests of the northern interior saw the first logging in the 1850s, when in the rush for gold, miners stripped the hillsides for mine timbers, housing and firewood. Large-scale logging did not begin until 1914, when the Grand Trunk Pacific railway was pushed north to Prince George. Spruce was in demand and the railway provided affordable access to markets to the south. During the eighty years since then, several types of harvest regimes were undertaken and, until recently, success with regenerating the forests was difficult.

The first loggers into the older, multi-aged stands of the sub-boreal forests practised partial cutting. This was largely due to the exclusive demand for prime spruce lumber, and up until the 1950s, only the spruce was harvested. The other species—lodgepole pine and subalpine fir—were left standing, and in many cases, were blown over by high winds. Loggers believed that the spruce would regenerate in

the stands and they could return later to harvest a second crop from the forest. Unfortunately, the spruce did not re-establish in the stands. In some cases only brush grew to replace the harvested spruce. In most other cases, subalpine fir, because it was more adapted to growing in the understorey, reclaimed the area the spruce had occupied. What were once mixed stands became pure fir stands.

In the early 1950s foresters began promoting clearcutting to ensure regeneration of spruce. Initially the clearcuts were made in an alternating pattern known as strip cutting. A strip of timber would be harvested while the adjacent strip would be left intact to seed the cut area. This system was used across the northern interior until the late 1960s.

The strip cutting system was phased out when foresters realized that regeneration in the harvested areas was too erratic to ensure future sustainability. In some cases brush would take over the sites so that new seedlings could not get established. In other cases too many trees regenerated and stands were overstocked and stagnant. While the concept of strip cutting looked good on paper, adequate overall regeneration was not being achieved. In addition, the strips left standing were being damaged by high winds, and salvage operations were necessary to save the affected timber.

In early 1970s, to better control regeneration, large-scale planting programs were started. By 1995, over 400 million trees had been planted and improvements in site preparation, nursery technology and planting timing were resulting in a survival rate of over 90 percent.

Forester Jim Burbee says that while regeneration is now generally successful, there are still occasions when his company has had to deal with brush competing with and overtaking the seedlings. He says current Forest Service regulations demand that brush be removed when it becomes a threat to seedling survival. In these cases, brush is controlled through the use of herbicides, sheep grazing or manual clearing. Burbee says that although all herbicides used on the forest are approved by many branches of government, they are used sparingly, and whenever possible, sheep grazing or manual brushing is used instead. He notes that in British Columbia in 1994, herbicides were used to control brush on only 12 percent of the area harvested.

To avoid the expense and delay in regeneration caused by brush competition, Burbee says his company tries to

BARKERVILLE 1868

In the 1860s, the town of Barkerville was the centre of a major gold rush. The hillside behind was logged for mine pit props and construction of buildings. In 1868, a major forest fire swept through the area, denuding the nearby forest.

(Below) Barkerville in 1994. The naturally regenerated forests are now mature.

BARKERVILLE 1994

offset the problem "by growing vigorous and robust seedlings that can compete better and not require as much site preparation.

"We're now at the point where we have a very effective plantation program," he adds, "and we're quite confident that we'll be able to re-establish a forest anywhere after harvesting."

While clearcutting is the most effective way of assuring good regeneration in the sub-boreal forest, recently foresters have modified their clearcuts to better mimic natural disturbances by wildfire and to provide increased diversity. Burbee explains that natural wildfires are strongly influenced by topography and generally follow the contour

of the land and leave scattered patches of unburned timber. Foresters are now doing much the same by shaping clearcuts to natural boundaries or landforms and leaving patches of standing timber within cutblocks. Wherever possible, these are designed to follow watercourses and avoid sensitive soil areas. The system is known as patch retention, and although modern clearcuts are much smaller than naturally burned areas, the system gives the appearance of a natural clearing by fire and is more acceptable to the general public. "The system really blends into the topography and changes the visual impact compared to a square clearcut," says Burbee. He notes that the "islands" of timber, which generally include both coniferous and deciduous trees, provide a

BARKERVILLE 1868

Since gold miners denuded the hills around Barkerville in the 1860s (left) nearby forests have enjoyed a century-and-a-quarter of undisturbed growth (below).

BARKERVILLE 1994

(Below) An experimental species plantation in the northern interior. This stand represents a provenance trial undertaken by forester John Revel (right). This provenance trial involves the growing of spruce trees from seed from many different interior locations to determine long-term genetic variability.

Current Forest Service regulations demand that brush be removed when it becomes a threat to seedling survival. In these cases, brush is controlled through the use of herbicides, sheep grazing, or manual clearing. Increasingly, sheep grazing or manual brushing is used. In British Columbia in 1994, herbicides were used to control brush on only 12 percent of the area harvested.

diversity of habitat for many nesting and perching animals, as well as visual screening for natural prey–predator relationships.

Burbee explains that because British Columbia's forest management is based on sustained yield, and cuts have to be balanced over a forest cycle of about 100 years, diversity was largely maintained in the past by providing for a variety of age classes ranging from new plantations and young forests to natural, old forests.

Bob Richards is a forester who has worked with the Forest Service in the Prince George Forest District for twenty-nine years. Richards says that in the past, there was little concern for biodiversity, particularly involving the small and large mammals that inhabit the forests. "When you have a huge clearcut, animals like the pine marten, which mainly lives in older, forested areas, are displaced, as are moose who need the cover during certain times of year."

Richards says that those concerns are now being addressed and animals protected under the ecosystem network guidelines of the Forest Practices Code. "When you log now, you leave a certain percentage of forested area which helps protect areas adjacent to streams and lakes. These are things that are being addressed."

Another concern is the retention of deciduous species within coniferous stands. "We've gone through the phase where we wanted to kill everything that wasn't a conifer," says Richards. "The leaves of the deciduous trees—especially trembling aspen—are high in nutrients and by having some of them in a stand, you get good nutrition added to the soil. We now know that we have to have some biodiversity of different species and we're trying more and more to move that way."

While regeneration after harvesting in the sub-boreal zone has not always been to man's satisfaction, nature

A lodgepole pine seedling. Over the past thirty years, over 400 million trees have been planted in the northern interior and the survival rate has reached over 90 percent.

assures that where the land is most suited to growing trees, trees will regenerate. As with all things in nature, in time those forests will die and a new generation will take their place. As man learns more about the importance of other values in the forest, he has adapted and changed his methods. Each year, more and more of those values are being considered and, although the working forest will never exactly mimic nature, foresters and wildlife biologists believe that most values can be maintained.

Forest Service employees Ken Pendergast (left) and Bob Richards examine a subalpine fir located within a mature portion of a strip-cutblock east of Prince George.
(Above) A landscape incorporating patch logging with areas of mature timber left to provide cover for wildlife and to protect riparian areas.

Twenty-year-old stands of lodgepole pine in the Ootsa Lake area.

The Truth In Numbers: The State of the Forests of the Northern Interior

The northern interior area of the province is encompassed by the Prince George Forest Region. The productive forests of this region contain 17.6 million hectares. Fifty-four percent (9.5 million hectares) is covered by mature forests. Of the remainder, 35 percent (6.2 million hectares) is made up of immature forests. Eleven percent of the area is classified as not-fully-stocked. In total, 89 percent of the productive forest land in the Prince George Forest Region is growing forests of various ages (see Appendix).

Between the years 1984 and 1994, the average annual harvesting effort involved 57,647 hectares. This represents just over one-half of 1 percent of the productive forest and less than one-quarter of the average of 254,047 hectares affected by wildfire and insects over the same time. Reforestation efforts saw the planting of over 94 million seedlings of nine different species in 1994.

Status of Productive Forest Land 1994

Prince George Forest Region • Total 17.6 million hectares

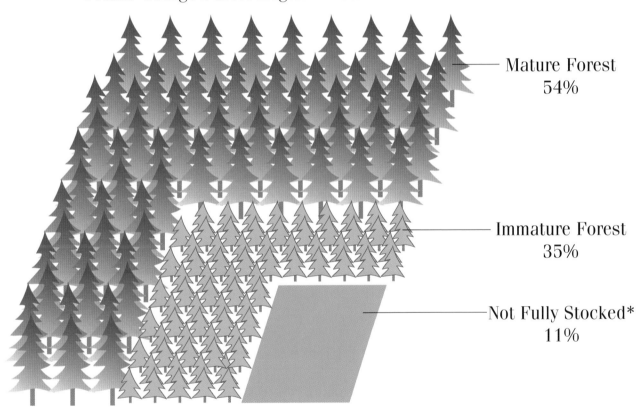

Mature Forest
54%

Immature Forest
35%

Not Fully Stocked*
11%

*includes areas denuded by fire and insects, stands of non-commercial trees and recent plantings.

Source: Ministry of Forests

The Largest Clearcut:
Bark Beetles in the Bowron

The dubious honour of being British Columbia's largest man-made clearcut belongs to the upper Bowron River watershed in the central portion of the province, fifty miles east of the city of Prince George. The operation grew to include a total of 52,500 hectares before it was finished, but it was far from the typical British Columbia clearcut it is often depicted as being. In fact it was a salvage operation made in response to a massive outbreak of the spruce bark beetle which killed millions of trees.

Problems began in the mid-1970s, when a series of storms and devastating winds resulted in numerous patches of blowdown in the Bowron watershed. Windfelled trees provide the ideal brood habitat for the spruce bark beetle, and populations soon increased to epidemic proportions. Much of the infestation was within the Bowron Lakes Provincial Park, an area known for its pristine wilderness values and a chain of lakes that offer generous canoe–camping opportunities. The Parks Branch did not want to see any harvesting of blowdown in the park and, as a result, the

In the early 1980s, it was apparent that drastic measures had to be taken to control the spread of spruce bark beetle infestation and reduce the risk of fire from the many dead trees. The Forest Service ordered the area to be cleared as quickly as possible. The extent of the damage was so great that all available logging and log hauling operators in the Prince George and Quesnel area were put to work on what became the most intense timber salvage operation in British Columbia history.

infestation continued unchecked for several years. The outbreak was further fuelled by extensive tracts of mature and overmature spruce stands and several mild winters which allowed insect populations to survive and then multiply exponentially.

In the early 1980s it was apparent that drastic measures had to be taken to control the spread of the infestation and reduce the risk of fire from the many dead trees. The Parks Branch agreed and the Forest Service ordered the area to be cleared as quickly as possible so that at least a portion of the value of the timber could be realized.

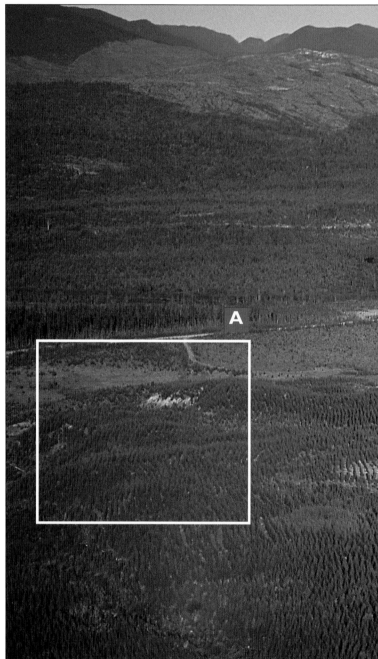

BOWRON
VALLEY
↓

A patch of natural blowdown in the Bowron Watershed. Windthrown trees provide the ideal brood habitat for the spruce bark beetle and populations soon increased to epidemic proportions.

A

Bowron Lakes, Northern Interior

Jim Burbee, chief forester for Northwood Pulp and Timber Co. Ltd., the lead company in the salvage operation, has returned many times to the areas which were clearcut and reports that they are now regenerating well. "Because the mature canopy is gone there are a lot more ground plants. The area is full of bears and they're flourishing on all the lush vegetation."

The extent of the damage was so great that all available logging and log hauling operators in the Prince George and Quesnel areas were put to work on what became the most intense timber salvage operation in British Columbia history. New roads were constructed so that workers could reach the dead, dying and threatened trees. Meanwhile, the infestation continued to spread.

By 1987, 52,500 hectares had been clearcut. Subsequently, well over 60 million spruce, lodgepole pine and Douglas fir seedlings were planted in the area.

Forester Jim Burbee believes that although many huge and unsightly clearcuts were made in the area, if the dead and dying timber had not been harvested, fire would eventually have swept through the dry wood and burned most of the affected area.

Burbee has returned many times to the areas that were clearcut and reports that they are now regenerating well. "Because the mature canopy is gone, there are a lot more ground plants. The area is full of bears and they're flourishing on all the lush vegetation." Burbee says that the person who holds the guiding rights to the area reports that black and grizzly bear populations have never been higher.

B

Bowron Lakes, Northern Interior

Bob Richards was also involved in the Bowron salvage operation. Although the operation was successful, he says opinion is divided on the control measures taken. "You will find people who are quite adamant that you can stop the beetle infestation, but I don't think that we ever really stopped it. I think that only Mother Nature stops infestations of this size. Eventually the population crashes because of natural mortality, whether it be their own diseases or parasites, or cold weather. I think we can control small infestations a fair bit—and we do that with 'trap' trees and different means—but I wouldn't say in the Bowron that we were controlling beetles, we were just salvaging timber." Richards says that although in 1981 the government and industry believed that the proper action was taken, in retrospect, he thinks the clearcut should not have been so extensive. "I don't think anyone can be proud of the vast clearcut up there. There could have been more reserves, more protection of riparian areas—even if the trees were going to die. In this day and age of wildlife concerns, bird concerns and protection of the water resources, to have a huge clearcut where there are no trees standing for 15 kilometres, I think it got a little bit out of hand."

Bowron Lakes,
Northern Interior

The forests are once again reclaiming the Bowron landscape. Well over 60 million spruce, lodgepole pine and Douglas-fir seedlings were planted in the Bowron clearcut.

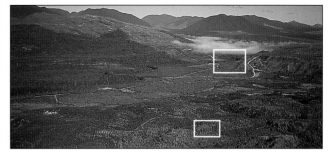

Bowron Lakes, Northern Interior

The timber adjacent to portions of the Bowron River was not harvested due to the important sockeye and spring salmon resources in the river (left). Beetle-killed trees can be seen in the lower left corner of the photo.

Two deer in a regenerated opening in the Bowron clearcut.

The Last Frontier:
The Forests of the North Coast

The final area of British Columbia's working forest to be visited begins at the Pacific Ocean, crosses the Coast Mountains and descends into the sub-boreal spruce and pine forests of the western part of the interior. The climate of the coastal portion of the region is dominated by mild temperatures and rain which changes to heavy snow and colder temperatures inland and on the higher-elevation mountains. Communities with a strong dependency on the forest industry include Prince Rupert, Terrace, Hazelton, Stewart, Smithers, Houston and Burns Lake.

The forests of this region are primarily coastal western hemlock and, in the higher elevations, mountain hemlock.

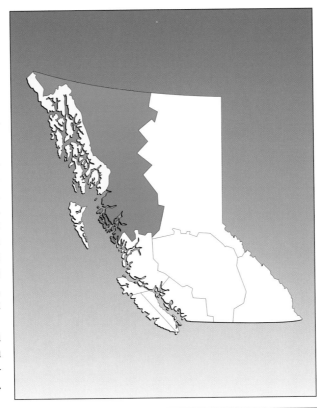

These two species, while of the same genus, are separate species and do not share the same growing sites except for a narrow transitional zone. Other species vary by climate and elevation, but include balsam, subalpine fir, yellow cedar, western red cedar, Sitka spruce and lodgepole pine. A unique natural hybrid spruce exists where the coastal Sitka spruce meets up with the interior white spruce. On the sheltered eastern portion of the mountains, the higher-elevation forests are characterized by the white spruce and subalpine fir zone. In the main river valleys of the Skeena, Nass and Stikine, extensive stands of deciduous black cottonwood grow in the rich alluvial soils.

Typical forested landscape north of Terrace in the Coastal Western Hemlock and Mountain Hemlock biogeoclimatic zones. Since the early 1900s, the forests of the valley have been providing logs for sawmills and a flourishing cedar pole industry.

Western hemlock, balsam and western red cedar are typical species of the North Coast's all-age, old-growth forests. Forests of the North Coast are not often exposed to large-scale catastrophic events such as blowdown, fire and/or insects. Instead, succession takes place when individual trees or groups of trees succumb to age and are replaced by young shade-tolerant species, such as hemlock.

The forest industry on the north coast of British Columbia was slow to develop due to the long distances and high cost of transporting products to markets. The first sawmills were built to supply ties to the Grand Trunk Railway being constructed from the interior to the coast city of Prince Rupert between 1908 and 1914. During the First World War, several small sawmills were constructed to supply lumber for the war effort. Sitka spruce, because of its strength and light weight, was most in demand. During the 1920s, the community of Terrace, located in the Skeena River valley halfway between the coast and the interior, became known as the "Pole Capital of the World" because of the abundance of western red cedar poles which were cut and shipped all over the world for telegraph and power transmission lines.

Large-scale forestry, however, didn't begin until 1948

Terrace is an example of the many BC communities which are dependent on the forest industry. Reflecting that dependency is this scene of sawmill, homes and businesses, with the combination of working forest and wilderness in the background.

with the granting of a Tree Farm Licence to Columbia Cellulose Company Ltd. near Prince Rupert. Under the old system, the government leased temporary cutting rights on Crown land to timber cutting companies. The new legislation gave some licensees secure, long-term cutting rights. In exchange, the licensees undertook responsibility for forest management, which included assurances that reforestation would occur.

One of the first foresters working on this TFL was Pem van Heek, who would later become landscape manager with the British Columbia Forest Service to develop many of the visual quality regulations for the forest industry today. Van Heek practised forestry for forty years.

He explains that during the early development of the TFL, clearcutting was the standard harvesting method and the average clearcut was about 40 hectares. Blocks of standing timber were left between the clearcuts to provide for natural regeneration. The majority of blocks regenerated well, with natural seedlings often reaching 2 metres in height six

years after logging, so thick it was difficult for a person to walk among them. At that time, slash burning and planting were not required by the BC Forest Service.

However, as more areas were logged and accumulations of slash grew, the Forest Service mandated that the slash be burned to reduce the summer fire hazard. Natural regeneration of conifers was not always successful in the wake of these burns, and supplementary planting was initiated. While the removal of ground cover by slash burning made the planting easier, many of the areas did not regenerate as well as expected—or even as well as the naturally regenerated areas that weren't burned.

Foresters were well aware that in the Douglas fir forests of the east coast of Vancouver Island and the Lower Mainland, fire has proven beneficial in regenerating the forests. This is because Douglas fir seedlings can withstand the higher ground temperatures that result from natural and man-made clearings. In most ecosystems, the seedlings need full sunlight to survive.

"Maybe we didn't do enough or maybe we weren't careful enough in the past, but now with reduced cuts and the Forest Practices Code, we are, I think, adapting to most public criticism."
Pem van Heek, *forester.*

Juvenile spacing of black cottonwood along the Nass River from approximately 5,000 stems per hectare (left) to 400 has resulted in strong volume growth on the remaining trees. Pem van Heek (above) with a stand of thinned thirty-five-year-old cottonwood.

In contrast, young hemlock and balsam prefer some shade and cooler ground temperatures. Burning results in full exposure to sunlight and high soil temperatures. During the first years of regeneration, this reduced survival rates of the seedlings of these species.

"If you burn everywhere, you can have troubles," says van Heek, "and we did run into troubles. In some areas we had to plant twice." He explains that there are pros (lower fire hazard and easier planting) and cons to slash burning. "For example, there are people who are very much against burning because it affects microorganisms in the humus layer and by doing so, you can set things back before they recover again." Today, professional foresters are much more careful in assessing whether burning is needed in each area or if some alternate form of site preparation can be used. Beginning in the late 1970s, a much wider range of mechanical site preparation equipment was becoming available. This, plus concerns about smoke pollution, have reduced the need for and limited prescribed burning. In 1994, controlled burning was used on less than 20 percent of the area harvested.

Another regeneration problem in coastal forests was caused by a little insect known as the Sitka spruce leader weevil which attacks young trees at ten to fifteen years. This weevil drills into the leaders of this species and causes stunted and distorted tree growth. So far, foresters and scientists have not been able to find a way around the spruce weevil and have instead adapted their planting practices.

While planting is not essential for regeneration from an ecological point of view, van Heek explains that the theory behind planting is to establish a new forest early and of equal or better quality than existed before harvesting. Over the years, foresters have calculated what they feel is the optimum spacing of seedlings to grow to their best potential. Too many surviving seedlings and the stand will become overcrowded and growth will slow down; too few and the site will not grow to its full potential.

While planting is undertaken on about half of British

By using a longline yarding system in Madsen Creek, part of TFL #1, workers can reach most timber while eliminating the visual and environmental impacts that can occur from logging roads built on steep slopes.

In the Terrace area, forester Erica Nicholson examines a naturally regenerated hemlock–balsam stand that was spaced in the 1980s.

Forester Archie McDonald takes a core sample of a balsam in a forty-two-year-old stand. Dense natural regeneration was juvenile spaced in the early 1980s and commercially thinned in 1994.

Columbia's harvested areas, foresters do not overlook the vital role of natural regeneration. It may not provide even distribution of seedlings, but their vitality and growth can be impressive. "I don't believe in the theory that if we plant so many trees per hectare the forest will be perfect and we can get the highest yield. I think we also have to work with systems using natural regeneration when appropriate."

Van Heek believes that the critics of forest practices have expressed some valid points. "Maybe we didn't have the knowledge or maybe we weren't careful enough in the past, but now with reduced cuts and the Forest Practices Code, we are, I think, adapting to most public criticism. The government is addressing the land use issue and many parks are being created. These are part of the concern of the public and I think this is positive and good. But in the remainder of the areas where we have good forest lands, and where the values are primarily for growing trees, there, I think, we should be free to grow these trees and make the land as productive as possible so it is beneficial to all of society, just as the parks are.

"I believe quite strongly in the recovery of natural systems," explains van Heek. "Sure, you can paint dark pictures and tell everybody ecological disasters are happening.

I'm not so quick to believe that. If you burned large areas and didn't plant or give them time to reforest, or if you changed the forest into rangeland, then you might change the ecological system and ecological balances too far. We keep on making sure the land is reforested. We have millions and millions of hectares of young forests growing and there are all kinds of wildlife and species being maintained. I don't think we are destroying species or the ecosystem."

The Truth In Numbers: The State of the Forests of the North Coast

The North Coast area of British Columbia is encompassed by the Prince Rupert Forest Region. The productive forests of this region cover 8.9 million hectares. Seventy-three percent (6.6 million hectares) is covered in mature forests. Of the remainder, 22 percent (2 million hectares) is made up of immature forests. Five percent of the area is classified as not-fully-stocked. In total, 95 percent of the productive forest of the Prince Rupert Forest Region is growing forests of various ages (see Appendix). During the ten-year period 1984–1994, the average harvesting effort involved 24,601 hectares annually. This represents just over one-quarter of 1 percent of the productive forest and compares to the average of 31,881 hectares affected by wildfire and insects over the same period. Reforestation efforts saw the planting of over 32 million seedlings of 12 different species in 1994.

Status of Productive Forest Land 1994

Prince Rupert Forest Region • Total 8.9 million hectares

Mature Forest
73%

Immature Forest
22%

Not Fully Stocked*
5%

*includes areas denuded by fire and insects, stands of non-commercial trees and recent plantings.

Source: Ministry of Forests

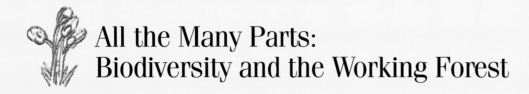

All the Many Parts:
Biodiversity and the Working Forest

British Columbia's diverse climate, topography and soils have produced a province which remains more biologically diverse, in terms of both species and ecosystems, than any other in Canada, according to the province's "1994 Forest, Range and Recreation Resource Analysis."

The report defines biological diversity (biodiversity) as "the variety of life and its processes," and is generally considered at three levels: genetic structure, species and ecosystem.

The analysis shows that British Columbia contains over half of the vascular plants estimated to occur in Canada as well as over 75 percent of the moss species, 85 percent of the lichen species and nearly all the species of liverworts and hornworts that inhabit northwestern North America.

The analysis also shows the richness of British Columbia's fauna parallels the richness of its flora. British Columbia has about 110 species of land-based mammals, nearly 80 percent of the Canadian total. It contains more large mammal species than any other province or state in North America. It has more than 70 percent of Canada's 454 bird species.

Even after the arrival of Europeans and almost 100 years of influence on the landscape by urban and rural development, mining, agriculture and forest harvesting, British Columbia continues to have not only the most diverse ecosystems, but also the most diverse flora and fauna in Canada.

"Many of these forests that we've been working in are ecologically in good condition," says Pem van Heek. "An old-growth forest has different birds and insects and life

Even after the arrival of Europeans and almost 100 years of influence on the landscape by urban and rural development, mining, agriculture and forest harvesting, British Columbia continues to have not only the most diverse ecosystems, but also the most diverse flora and fauna in Canada.

Tree frog.

Western painted turtles.

A young bull moose in a clearing.
British Columbia contains more large mammal species
than any other province or state in North America.

systems than a young, new forest. After harvesting, changes occur. Because there is more browse, more deer and more grouse are present than in the old forest. Eventually these animals will go somewhere else because the forest becomes so dense that the food supply is diminished. The ecological balances are always changing, whether it is a natural forest or a plantation."

Bill Dumont believes that biodiversity has more to do with habitat than with species. "If you have the habitat, the species will be there. That's the thinking of biologists today. If you can protect the habitat you'll have your species. I

maintain that we have not lost a single species to logging and the habitat is actually far more diverse than before we arrived—and that to me is a pretty good indication that the species richness and health is still very good after eighty years of development."

One of British Columbia's thinkers on the effects of the forest harvesting on the environment is Dr. Hamish Kimmins, a professor of forest ecology at the University of British Columbia. In his book *Balancing Act*, Kimmins says that the diversity of plant species in temperate forests changes constantly. "Clearcutting—or fire or wind or

Forester Bill Dumont believes that biodiversity has more to do with habitat than with species. "If you have the habitat, the species will be there. That's the thinking of biologists today... I maintain that we have not lost a single species to logging and the habitat is actually far more diverse than before we arrived— and that to me is a pretty good indication that the species richness and health is still very good after eighty years of development."

Wood lily

Bobcat

disease disturbances—increases some aspects of diversity and decreases others," he says. "For animal species, the cycle of change often follows the same pattern, with different animal species thriving or dwindling as a particular stand passes through all the stages of its existence."

Kimmins says many plant species are adapted to the creation, whether natural or man-made, of sudden openings in the forest, and some could not survive without them. "Although there are species that can adapt to every phase of the forest cycle, other plants and animals thrive best in recent openings. While some plant and animal species depend on old growth, others cannot survive in it."

Critics of clearcut logging have expressed concern over the potential loss of biodiversity and the creation of monoculture forests when cutblocks are planted. Without doubt some plantations are monocultural, but then so are some wild stands. Mature Douglas fir and lodgepole pine, for example, are often found in pure stands. After logging,

(Top) Shooting star.

(Centre) Fireweed is one of the species that quickly occupies many clearcut areas.

(Below) Huckleberry.

the same species which were removed from a site are plant-ed and, according to Professor Kimmins, "the resultant sec-ond crop may become a pure stand, which is environmen-tally acceptable." Kimmins says that there is a high, natur-al tree-to-tree genetic diversity in coniferous forests due to wind pollination. When combined with seeds already in the forest floor (or blown in from another forest), seedlings already growing, and seedlings planted by foresters, the genetic characteristics of the original forest are contained

Willow ptarmigan.

Porcupine.

Wood duck.

"Clearcutting—or fire or wind or disease disturbances—increases some aspects of diversity and decreases others. For animal species, the cycle of change often follows the same pattern, with different animal species thriving or dwindling as a particular stand passes through all the stages of its existence."
Dr. Hamish Kimmins, *professor of forest ecology, University of British Columbia, in his book* Balancing Act.

British Columbia has more than 70 percent of Canada's 454 bird species. (Right) Ring-necked pheasant.

and maintained in the new trees. In addition, the wide variety of seed collection sites assures that species genetic diversity is maintained.

David Handley says that despite the early practice of planting only Douglas fir on Vancouver Island, nature has ensured that the stands are biologically diverse. "You can go almost anywhere and you'll find a variety of species, and where you don't find a variety of species, it usually means that only one species will grow well on that site. I believe that none of our forests have more or less variety today than 100 years ago."

Handley says MacMillan Bloedel has studied the progress of its second growth since the early 1950s. "You can look at new forests almost anywhere in the province and find more than one tree species grow-

ing together. On those areas where this is not the case, it is usually because only one species is ecologically well adapted to the conditions. Some new forests have more tree diversity than the predecessor forest did; in some cases it is the reverse. This is a reflection of the random and opportunistic way nature manages."

No one knows exactly what effect natural disturbances had on biodiversity during the thousands of years prior to European settlement. What is certain is that despite catastrophic fires, blowdown, insect infestations and landslides that have affected virtually every hectare of British Columbia at one time or another, the diversity of species and ecosystems regained equilibrium. The disruptions added by man over the past 100 years have not altered that diversity.

(Above) The gray jay is also known as the whiskey jack.

The diversity of species and ecosystems as we see them today has endured despite catastrophic fires, blowdown, insect infestations and landslides that have affected virtually every hectare of British Columbia at one time or another. The impact of timber harvesting fits well within this history of disruption.

The Status of British Columbia's Forests

In 1994, Ministry of Forests statistics showed that British Columbia contained 45.7 million hectares of productive forest land, 26 million of which was in the working forest. Mature forests covered 59 percent (26.9 million hectares) while immature forests covered 34 percent (15.5 million hectares). Seven percent of the area was in recent plantings, non-commercial species, brush and areas denuded by natural disturbances and harvesting, all of which the ministry classified as not-fully-stocked.

The remaining 93 percent of British Columbia's productive forest land was growing forests of various ages. For the ten-year period 1984 to 1994, an average of 224,000 hectares were harvested each year. This represented less than 1 percent of the productive forest. Over the same period, wildfire and insects affected an average of 820,000 hectares each year—over three times the amount harvested by the forest industry. Throughout British Columbia, reforestation efforts saw the planting of over 210 million seedlings of 18 different species in 1994 (see Appendix).

Status of Productive Forest Land 1994

British Columbia • Total 45.7 million hectares

Mature Forest
59%

Immature Forest
34%

Not Fully Stocked*
7%

*includes areas denuded by fire and insects, stands of non-commercial trees and recent plantings.

Source: Ministry of Forests

PART THREE

*Second-growth forests have reclaimed the landscape
devastated by the massive 1938 Sayward fire.*

Before A Single Tree Falls:
The Planning Process

As in most endeavours in life, planning is a very necessary function in the field of forestry. In British Columbia, before a single tree can be harvested on public land (94 percent of BC), a rigorous process of assessment and planning must be undertaken, presented to the public for comment and approved by the BC Forest Service. In most cases, this takes up more time than the actual harvesting operation itself and begins up to five years ahead of time. While responsibility for the assessment and planning process varies according to the type of tenure—in some cases the Forest Service undertakes the task, in others the forest industry is responsible—it is important to realize that all forest tenures in British Columbia are obligated to conduct the same process of planning and approvals. British Columbia is one of the world leaders in the level of detail it requires.

An example of the planning process can be illustrated through the regulations governing Tree Farm Licences—areas of land owned by the British Columbia government, but where the right to manage and harvest its forest resources are granted to a forest company for twenty-five years.

The process begins with the preparation of a five-year Management Plan. A Management Plan sets the strategic direction for the management of the tenure area, delineating the geographic, biological and climatic conditions affecting the area, and identifying the tree species that grow there. It forecasts the allowable annual cut, or quota, based on predictions as far as 200 years into the future, and sets out the proportions of natural regeneration and planting that will be needed to keep the resource restocked to the levels required by the Forest Service. It must also include plans to minimize the impact of its operations on other resource values.

The draft document is made available to all interested parties and other resource users in the area. This may include First Nations groups, ranchers, commercial fishermen, trappers, hunting guides, fishing camp operators and government officials of the federal Department of Fisheries and Oceans and the provincial Fish and Wildlife Branch of the Ministry of Environment, Lands and Parks. It is also presented to the general public through round-table discussions and open houses. The Management Plan is then revised to take into account any concerns raised during these public consultations and finally submitted to the Forest Service. If the plan complies with the Forest Practices Code, the government foresters may approve it, or—if they disagree with the approach or conclusion—the Management Plan may be sent back to the appropriate government or industry foresters for redrafting. When the plan is finally approved, the BC Forest Service makes a decision on how much timber can be harvested from the tenure for the ensuing five years.

≺ *A mix of both old-growth and regeneration after logging in the Kamloops area*

Traditionally, stands harvested in the BC interior were left to regenerate naturally. Today there is an increasing trend toward replanting cut blocks immediately after harvesting.

A

For the public, the aesthetics of cutblocks are important,
so clearcuts in many areas are irregularly shaped and
relatively small. At Jamieson Creek, clearcuts are no
more than 14 hectares and within each area, pockets of
trees are left standing, including those that crown the
tops of ridges (above). The logged area in the foreground
was drag scarified to prepare the site for replanting.

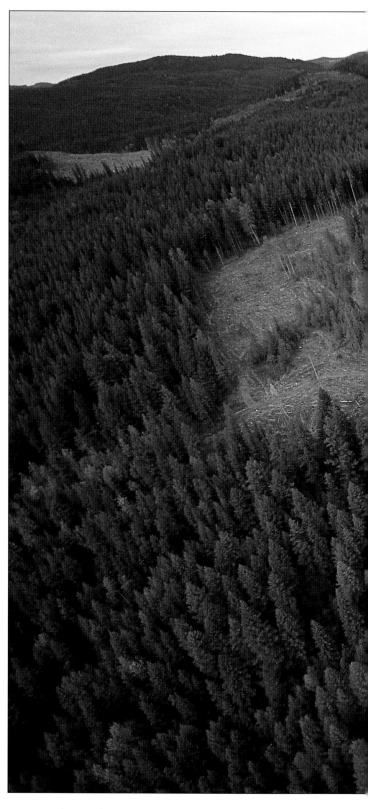

"Natural restocking on our sites, and with our native
species, only produced 75 percent of the yield of
planted stands, therefore we plant all sites.
I believe that good, basic forestry practices—
plant with vigorous seedlings of the proper species for
the site, and with spacing to a target level—should
increase allowable cuts in BC by at least 30 percent."
Steve Tolnai, forester.

Weyerhaeuser senior foresters Les Laithwaite (left) and Steve Tolnai at Jamieson Creek.

Harvesting methods vary at Jamieson Creek—both partial cutting and small-scale clearcutting are used—and rubber-tired, mechanized logging equipment with low ground pressure reduces the effects on soils. The area shown in the photo above was partially cut. A number of the larger interior Douglas fir trees were left as seed trees. Some deciduous trees were also left standing.

One of the partial cutting systems used at Jamieson Creek.

With the Management Plan providing a strategic framework, the foresters now narrow their focus to creating five-year Development Plans for individual areas within the tenure. A Development Plan is a precise blueprint that identifies the specific stands of timber to be cut during the five years, and the sequence in which the cutting will take place, the methods that will be used to build and maintain logging roads, the harvesting equipment and techniques to be applied, fire protection and reforestation plans, and the measures that will prevent, minimize or mitigate environmental disturbances. In some cases, the plan will involve the preservation or deferral of stands on very steep slopes, for wildlife habitat, and along streams, seashores and lakes. Other provisions call for re-establishing natural drainage flows, and breaking up the surfaces of roads, then recontouring, seeding and planting so they will blend back into the landscape. The harvesting plans will consider the aesthetics of the working forest: the siting and design of cutblocks will take into account how they will appear to people using nearby highways, lakes, and recreation areas. The

Development Plan goes into detail in providing for the protection of archaeological and historic sites, and ensuring that forestry and other resource uses can co-exist.

As with the Management Plan, putting together the Development Plan is a public process. But instead of a general consultation, foresters now work with individual stakeholders who will be specifically affected by their operations, to ensure that there is minimal conflict among users of the forests. Again, the Development Plan, which is signed by a forester, is not complete until it has been evaluated and approved by the Forest Service and the Ministry of Environment, Lands and Parks.

The Development Plan is by no means the final stage of planning. When it is completed, the focus narrows even further, and foresters must develop Silvicultural Prescriptions (SPs) for individual harvesting sites. A Silvicultural Prescription begins two or three years before the tree fallers arrive, with foresters studying the site to collect data on soil types and conditions, plant and wildlife populations, the characteristics of the terrain and the extent of its water resources.

For ranchers in the interior, the concern is the availability of open land with sufficient forage for their herds, so foresters have to ensure that harvesting and reforestation operations do not put barriers in the way of free-ranging cattle nor diminish their food supply.

This plan must be signed and sealed by a forester, and its quality is the mark by which its preparer will be judged by other professionals. It is an explicit document that identifies the resources on a specific few hectares; it defines the harvesting methods down to the details of the equipment that will be employed and the season of harvest; it stipulates the reforestation procedures, from site preparation to the species to be planted, to stems per hectare stocking standards; and it sets out the particular measures to be used to mitigate environmental impacts and protect fish and wildlife resources.

The manner in which the working forest is tended depends upon all of the many factors and relationships that come into play when science, nature and human priorities intermix. Foresters must take into account the other four main uses of the working forest: recreation, tourism, wildlife and, in the interior of the province, ranching.

An example of the planning process can be seen in the Jamieson Creek drainage that forms the bulk of Tree Farm Licence #35 held by Weyerhaeuser Canada Ltd. TFL #35 covers 36,400 hectares of range and timber land 28 kilometres north of the city of Kamloops in the high, dry central interior. Here the planning process is overseen by Weyerhaeuser's senior foresters, Steve Tolnai, Bob Helfrich

"Not only is the working forest being renewed, it is being managed to yield higher volumes of timber than came out of the original stands, while at the same time respecting other forest values, like water, wildlife and recreation."
Les Laithwaite, *forester.*

(Above) These special pine trees are used for seed production to supply Weyerhaeuser's seedling nursery.

A white spruce seedling (left). Over 210 million seedlings of 18 different species were planted in BC in 1994.

and Les Laithwaite. In addition to the steps outlined above, other special considerations are taken into account. For the public, the aesthetics of cutblocks are important, so clearcuts at Jamieson Creek are irregularly shaped and relatively small—no larger than 14 hectares—and within each area, pockets of trees are left standing, including those that crown the tops of ridges. For ranchers, the concern is the availability of open land with sufficient forage for their herds, so foresters have to ensure that harvesting and reforesting operations do not put barriers in the way of free-ranging cattle nor diminish their food supply.

Harvesting methods vary at Jamieson Creek—both partial cutting and small-scale clearcutting are used—and rubber-tired, mechanized logging equipment with low ground pressure minimizes the harm to soils. Only 1 percent of the tenure is logged each year; since most cutblocks are planted the season after logging. That means 98 percent of the land is always in some stage of its life cycle as a productive forest.

The lodgepole pine seedlings—grown to an age of one or two years in the Weyerhaeuser nursery from seed collected in the same area—are often placed near stumps or logs to protect them from damage by roaming cattle. When necessary, competing brush is removed after planting, and

(Above) A lodgepole pine plantation showing good regeneration after eight years.

(Left) Weyerhaeuser's seedling nursery.

the juvenile crop is later spaced, if necessary, to encourage larger and higher-quality trees.

The result is a highly successful working forest, with stem counts on planted land averaging 1,600 to 2,500 young trees per hectare—far above the level required by legislation—as well as consideration of the needs of tourists, ranchers and First Nations. The unique distribution of age classes coupled with the opportunity to maximize intensive forest management practices at Jamieson Creek has led to it being one of the only tenures in British Columbia whose allowable annual cut has been increased by the Forest Service.

Another example of the rigorous planning process that occurs in British Columbia can be seen in the Nahmint Valley. The Nahmint is a narrow valley between steep mountain slopes 20 kilometres southwest of the mill town of Port Alberni. Along its bottom, finger-shaped Nahmint Lake drains into a turbulent river connecting it to Alberni Inlet, which finally winds down to the Pacific Ocean at Barkley Sound. The water is full of fish—salmon, steelhead, cutthroat trout and Dolly Varden char—and the woods are home to deer, elk, cougar and bear.

The Nahmint also holds some 12,000 hectares of mature coniferous forest—Douglas fir, western red cedar, western hemlock and balsam—all part of a forest tenure held by MacMillan Bloedel Limited. Most of the world is now aware of Clayoquot Sound and the rigorous provisions that have been made to limit the impact of harvesting in that prized recreational area. Those inclined to think of this as a first in British Columbia forest practice might be surprised to find that the forest industry has been responding to sensitive areas at least since 1975, when the Nahmint Valley on Vancouver Island's Alberni Inlet was first designated a special integrated-use area.

In 1975, provincial Chief Forester Bill Young decreed that the Nahmint would be a test case for a new policy, called Integrated Resource Management (IRM). MacMillan Bloedel's foresters would have to design patterns and levels of timber harvesting that would take into account the many other resource users in the valley. In 1990, the government updated and broadened its fifteen-year-old studies and reclassified the working forest of the Nahmint as an area for low-intensity harvesting: uses like wildlife preservation, fishing and recreation would have a higher priority than the timber harvest.

Every stage of the planning process used for other tenures, from Management Plan to Development Plan to Silvicultural Prescription, also applies to the management of the Nahmint Valley, but above and beyond the province-wide standards imposed by the Forest Act, there are extra restrictions on the use of the working forest in these 20,000 hectares of rugged wilderness.

The Nahmint River as it passes through a narrow canyon.

"BC's forest management is as good as, if not better than, most forest jurisdictions in the world. The unique nature of our forests—climates, terrains, the types and distribution of species, site characteristics and non-timber values, make comparisons with any other country's forestry operations meaningless. But our uniqueness does provide the opportunity to obtain the necessary balance that produces a sustainable forest environment and economic benefits for society."
Jim MacFarlane, *forester.*

◄ *The mouth of the Nahmint River where it joins the Pacific Ocean on southern Vancouver Island. The harvesting standards are special here because the place is special.*

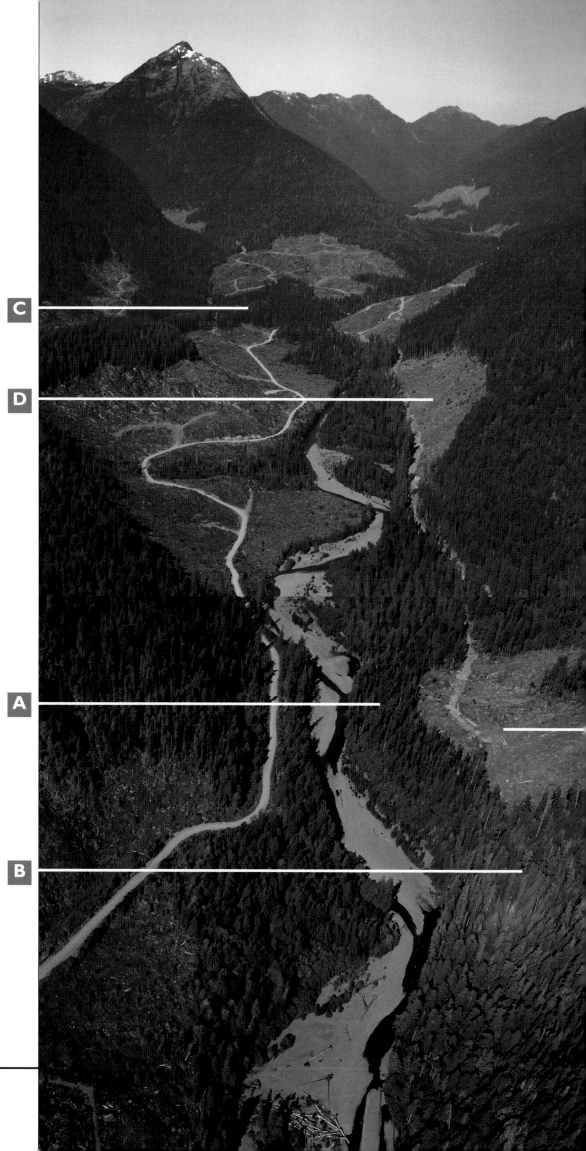

The Nahmint has a wider variety of plant and animal species than is found in most valleys. Sartisohn and MB's forest managers employ an elaborate computer modelling system to simulate the various ecosystems and decide which harvesting techniques and schedules will lead to the best net outcome for all of the values to be found in the regenerated forest.

An experimental cutblock in the Nahmint Valley. The landscape shown here incorporates irregular cutblock sizes throughout, buffer zones to protect salmon habitat (a), intact old-growth (b), and continuous wildlife corridors throughout (c). Cutblocks are smaller (d)— no more than 20 hectares— and carefully shaped and sited to soften their outlines when viewed by anglers and boaters on the lake.

C

D

A

B

A truckload of logs leaving the Nahmint Valley.

Gabriela Sartisohn, MB's area forester, ensures that the Nahmint receives special handling, which makes for a sophisticated professional challenge.

This former logging access road was deactivated. When a road is deactivated the ditches are cleaned out and trenches are cut into the road to assist with natural drainage. Sometimes culverts and bridges are also removed

Helicopter logging (above and below), although expensive, is being used on some slopes in the Nahmint to prevent the soil damage that may result from roadbuilding.

Finger-shaped Nahmint Lake drains into the river that bears the same name, connecting to Alberni Inlet, which finally winds down to the Pacific Ocean at Barkley Sound. The water is full of fish—salmon, steelhead, cutthroat trout and Dolly Varden char. Feeder streams and the Nahmint River itself are protected by strips of timber left standing on their banks.

The standards are special because the place is special and plans for harvesting, reforestation and silvicultural operations must be approved by a committee made up of people representing other resource interests such as First Nations, tourism, and fish and wildlife organizations.

Gabriela Sartisohn, MB's area forester, ensures that the Nahmint receives special handling, which makes for a sophisticated professional challenge. Helicopter logging, although expensive, is being used on some slopes to prevent the soil damage that may result from roadbuilding. Cutblocks are smaller—no larger than 20 hectares—and carefully shaped and sited to soften their outlines when viewed by anglers and boaters on the lake. Streams are protected by strips of timber left standing on their banks, and wildlife corridors from valley bottom to mountaintop ensure cover for species that need mature forests. Preserving biodiversity is a complex matter: the Nahmint has a wider variety of plant and animal species than is found in most valleys. Sartisohn and MB's forest managers employ an elaborate computer modelling system to simulate the various ecosystems and decide which harvesting techniques and

schedules will lead to the best net outcome for all of the values to be found in the regenerated forest.

Reforestation involves a mixture of planting and natural regeneration. As at Jamieson Creek, seedlings are given a boost by the removal of competing brush, at an early age, to ensure that they reach the stage foresters call "free growing." The southern reaches of the valley were planted in Douglas fir, western red cedar, balsam and western hemlock in 1979 and 1980; by 1994 the trees were more than 6 metres tall—much higher than most stands of their age.

While Jamieson Creek and the Nahmint are both special cases in terms of the degree of forest management planning that has been put into them, in another way they are typical of the approach being taken to all sites today and on all tenures. Throughout British Columbia, as special values are identified, they are incorporated into harvesting plans. In some sense each and every site is assumed to have a unique ecological character that must be respected and preserved. Some require more special treatment than others, but all are subject to a sophisticated process designed to assure their unique needs are identified and met.

Although logging has taken place in the Nahmint Valley for almost eighty years, the forests have regenerated well.

PART FOUR

*A landscape of mature and immature timber
in the working forest north of Kamloops
in the province's interior.*

A Matter of Choices:
The Future of the Working Forest

*A*t the beginning, *The Working Forest of British Columbia* set out to examine the state of the province's working forest. Many concerns have been raised about the effects of over 100 years of commercial harvesting of British Columbia's trees, the main ones being: how much of the forest is left, and how successfully is the old-growth being replaced by new stands? The aim of the book was to visit the actual sites where harvesting has taken place so readers could see the answers to these questions with their own eyes. Along the way, the book investigated such related issues as the role of natural disturbance on the forest, how man-made disturbance relates to natural disturbance, the history and present state of forest management in British Columbia, and the place of non-timber values in today's working forest.

Given the vibrant second-growth stands found in all forest regions, the results of the book's visual survey can only be regarded as positive. After a century or more of commercial harvesting, over 90 percent of the province's forest lands are still growing trees. There have been places where management was not what it could have been, but the forest ecosystem has such a natural capacity to thrive on major disturbance, most of those places have recovered well.

Foresters have been planning harvesting operations and monitoring environmental impacts for nearly fifty years, but to outside eyes, the province's long-established plan to convert the working portion of its forest to a sustainable managed forest can be mistaken for no plan at all. In part, this is because of the vast scale on which operations are carried out. Since the early 1900s, foresters have been forced to deal with their responsibilities in broad strokes. The forest was so huge and the population so sparse that the intensive tree-by-tree approach taken by more settled countries was not an option. The large scale of the harvest has tended to obscure the equally large scale of the reforestation program. As British forester Jack Harrison said after accompanying a UK delegation to investigate British Columbia forest practices in 1994, "It is difficult for us, living in a small country with small timber holdings, to grasp the immensity of this country with its vast forests and wildlife until we see it with our own eyes. It is truly magnificent."

Laying aside the past, the intensification of forest management taking place in British Columbia in the 1990s is unmistakable. There are over 3,000 foresters working in every forest area in the province, carrying out more rigorously than ever their commitment to sustainable forestry for all users. The kind of planning viewed in visits to the Nahmint Valley and Jamieson Creek reveals such a highly developed process it moved President Klepsch of the European Parliament to say, "Your work on environmental issues should be a model for Europe." The additional thrust of the 1995 Forest Practices Code has increased the degree of regulation considerably—beyond even that witnessed by Dr. Klepsch.

Despite strong management efforts, questions remain about the sustainability of the British Columbia timber supply due to so-called "falldown" and "netdown" effects. Some critics believe that the timber yield will drop substantially when the bulk of the harvest is second-growth rather than old-growth, but others argue there could be an increase in productivity. Senior foresters like Dick Kosick report that after growing only sixty years, some second-growth plantations are producing nearly as much volume as old-growth cut on the same land.

In any case, if we take advantage of the faster growth rates of younger trees over a growing period of eighty to one hundred years, long-term productivity can be much higher despite the smaller size of individual trees. This is the principle followed in longer-established forest economies like Sweden's, where forests continue to support a productive and competitive forest industry and increasing allowable cuts, despite many crop rotations.

It is important to realize that the magnificent 500-year-old stands of giant trees existed only on the coast and were not to be found everywhere, even there. In the interior, where 70

◄ *A young forest on the Tofino flats of the west coast of Vancouver Island that regenerated after harvesting, slash-burning and planting in 1971.*

percent of the timber harvest takes place, preserving ancient old-growth stands is not the same issue. Major species like lodgepole pine mature at eighty years and in the past were frequently prevented from reaching even that age by pervasive wildfire and insect infestation. Whereas man has reduced the age of the coast forest, in the interior he may have made the forest older. Thanks to improved wildfire control, some foresters say the average age of the interior's mature forests is greater now than it was at the turn of the century.

Because the forests of the interior of the province become overmature and begin deteriorating so much more quickly than coastal forests, much of the old growth is decadent and probably would have burned off if not for improved fire suppression by government and industry. When this decadent timber is replaced with new managed stands, forest planners believe yields of sound wood in the interior will increase markedly.

Relative to the productivity of young stands, Gerry Burch states, "The final challenge is the potential for increasing the yields of our immature forests on a shrinking land base. The new practices that are being considered are juvenile stand spacing, commercial thinning, fertilization and the valuable role of forest genetics. The important policy decisions that must be made are: Who will carry out these practices? What areas or stands justify the expense? And who will pay the costs involved? There is no doubt that foresters believe these intensive forestry practices can greatly affect allowable cuts in the long run. The adoption of the Forest Renewal program in 1995 will stimulate the funds needed to carry out intensive forest programs throughout the province and increase productivity."

While the jury is still out on the "falldown" effect, there is no mistaking the "netdown" effect, which occurs when productive forest land is removed from the working forest for other uses: parks, hydroelectric reservoirs and rights-of-way, highways, residential development, native land claims settlements, environmental protection and other uses. Some foresters have calculated that the 1995 Forest Practices Code alone will reduce the allowable cut of the working forest by an estimated 6 percent. Further, the total netdown caused by the provincial government's CORE process, the Protected Areas Strategy for doubling British Columbia parklands, and the Forest Practices Code, has been estimated at over 25 percent.

While the falldown effect can be offset by increased silvicultural effort and more efficient technology, the netdown effect is not under the industry's control and may well present the more serious threat to British Columbia's position as a leading timber producer in the world.

Uncertainty about the eventual size of the working forest is one of the major impediments to the new generation of foresters as they face the future. One of those foresters is Les Skaalid, who has twelve years of experience with Finlay Forest Industries Ltd. in northern British Columbia. Says Skaalid: "Obviously, different people have different thoughts on what the forest should be like and what benefits they should derive. That is one of the biggest concerns we as young foresters have. Land use decisions are not for one group to make. The public, government and industry are going to have to get together to make these decisions. There has to be a higher-level plan that designates areas that should be set aside as parks and wilderness and, at the same time, gives direction to the industry on the area that will comprise the working forest. We're spending millions of dollars upgrading facilities to achieve better utilization and trying to keep them and our communities viable. We can't keep making valley-by-valley decisions based on controversy. This is the main problem with forestry today and probably the biggest challenge to all parties concerned."

Unfortunately, the assumptions on which some members of the public base their opinions that the working forest should be downsized *are* the result of misunderstanding. One of the most common arguments for withdrawing land from the working forest assumes that timber harvesting is incompatible with recreational activities. But statistics gathered by the Ministry of Forests show that 84 percent of forest recreation takes place on land previously affected by timber harvesting. This is due in part to improvements such as roads, trails, canoe routes, campsites and better public information. Another reason given for removing lands from the working forest is wildlife protection. But senior foresters such as Trevor Jeanes and Dick Kosick point out

that like wildfire and other natural disturbances, logging can provide essential habitat variety for many forms of wildlife.

In recent years, perhaps the most determined opposition to timber harvesting activity in British Columbia has been waged on environmental grounds. Ecological arguments have been made that forest practices are not compatible with ecosystem integrity and biological diversity. These arguments are challenged by authorities like Prof. Hamish Kimmins of the UBC Faculty of Forestry, who argue that typical British Columbia forest practices such as clearcutting are compatible with good ecosystem management when used appropriately. Also, the oft-made claim by those opposed to logging that managed forests are barren monocultures is incorrect. Most second-growth forests support a range of species almost equivalent to that of old-growth forests.

In some respects the managed forest protects the environment better than natural processes. The huge wildfires that used to incinerate thousands of hectares at a time are far fewer in the managed forest. Between 1920 and 1930, wildfires burned an average of 220,000 hectares per year. Modern control programs had reduced the impact of fires to 55,000 hectares per year between 1984 and 1994. The reduction is substantial and is nearly equal to the annual area harvested.

In the end, all the working forest needs to flourish is a policy of enlightened and evolving forest management. With that, there is no reason the province's fertile growing sites cannot continue supporting magnificent forests and satisfying the world's demand for quality wood products. Seeing this through is one of the challenges facing young foresters today. Says Skaalid: "Today we are dealing with total resource planning—integrating all the concerns of the forest ecosystem as a whole. We work with the Ministry of Environment in considering wildlife, fish and water resources. We deal with resource users like trappers and guides and address their concerns by making sure that there is enough cover and corridors for wildlife. Another important concern is visual aesthetics—what the landscape looks like—and we use digital terrain modelling to plan our cutblocks so they have the best visual impact. We are trying to be responsive to the concerns of all the other users of the forest, and to keep them informed about what we are trying to do." Skaalid notes that when these concerns are taken seriously, there is less criticism of forest policies, and a much better working relationship with the people who live in the area.

Skaalid adds: "I believe that the forest industry has a great future in BC. There are a number of incentives going on right now, like the Forest Renewal program which will help with better inventories, reclamation projects and intensive silviculture. The industry is looking at increasing utilization of the harvested logs and also more intensive silviculture. These are things that will be ongoing."

Don Couch has been a forester with Riverside Forest Products Limited in the southern interior of the province for sixteen years. He is another of the younger generation of foresters who are managing today's forests for the future. "I think the future has a lot of opportunities," says Couch. "We're much more sophisticated than we've ever been before, and we will continue to get more sophisticated and to diversify and add value to the products we produce. Our scientific knowledge is increasing and this gives us a better understanding about ecosystems and how they respond to forest practices. We're also able to monitor what we do and establish better standards.

"What we did five years ago is different than what we do today," he adds. "What we did ten years ago was different, and what we did when I first started working in the woods as a kid was very different than what we do today. In the next five years, we're not sure what we're going to be doing, what those changes are, but we do know it is going to be different."

Couch concludes: "We're doing the best we can and, because in any one year we're only harvesting less than 1 percent of the land base, the impact we're having is minute. We can see what happens over time and we can make necessary adjustments when we see the need, or when society sees the need.

"I am confident that as society's values for the forest adapt and change over time, so will we in the industry adapt and change."

APPENDIX
Note on Statistics

Most figures used in this book were obtained from BC Ministry of Forests Annual Reports for the years 1984–1994 and the 1994 Forest, Range & Recreation Resource Analysis, also published by the Ministry of Forests. The following notes apply to those figures.

It is important to bear in mind that not all productive forest land is operable, economic and therefore available. The total productive and operative forest land in British Columbia is 26,000,000 hectares, or 47 percent of the total forested area of British Columbia.

Figures may not add due to rounding.

Immature stands are defined as those stands with lodgepole pine and whitebark pine or deciduous species as the leading species which are age 80 or less. When greater than 80 years, the stand is classified as mature. All other stands are immature when the stand age is 120 years or less. When the stand is greater than 120 years, the stand is classified as mature.

Immature forests include areas of natural disturbances and/or timber harvesting.

Not-fully-stocked areas include areas denuded by natural disturbances, harvested areas planted but not yet classified as "free growing," and stands of non-commercial species, generally deciduous. Due to the time period between harvest and the free-growing stage—between five and seven years—there will always be an area of NFS equivalent to the area harvested over those years.

Major forest insects are bark beetles and insect defoliators.

Figures for the total area annually affected by naturally occurring blowdown, snowdown, avalanches and landslides were not available or factored into these figures.

SELECTED BIBLIOGRAPHY

British Columbia. Ministry of Forests. *Forest, Range & Recreation Resource Analysis, 1994*. Victoria: Ministry of Forests, 1995.

British Columbia. Ministry of Forests. *Ministry of Forests Management of Forest Service Recreation Sites: A Public Preference Study*. Victoria: Ministry of Forests, Recreation Branch, 1992.

British Columbia. Royal Commission on Forest Resources. *Timber Rights and Forest Policy*. Report of the Royal Commission on Forest Resources, Peter H. Pearse, Commissioner, 1976.

Council of Forest Industries of British Columbia. *British Columbia Forest Industry Fact Book: 1994*. Vancouver: Council of Forest Industries of British Columbia, 1994.

Drushka, Ken. *Stumped: The Forest Industry in Transition*. Vancouver: Douglas & McIntyre Ltd., 1985.

Drushka, Ken. *Working in the Woods*. Maderia Park, BC: Harbour Publishing, 1992.

Farley, A.L. *Atlas of British Columbia: People, Environment and Resource Use*. Vancouver: University of British Columbia Press, 1979.

Halleran, Mike. *Loggers and Lumbermen: The Evolution of the Forest Industry in the Southern Interior of British Columbia*. Kelowna, BC: The Interior Lumber Manufacturers' Association, 1994.

Harding, Lee E. and Emily McCullum. *Biodiversity in British Columbia: Our Changing Environment*. Victoria: Environment Canada and Canadian Wildlife Service, 1994.

Kimmins, J.P. *Balancing Act: Environmental Issues in Forestry*. Vancouver: University of British Columbia Press, 1992.

Krajina, V., K. Klinka and J. Worrall. *Distribution and Ecological Characteristics of Trees and Shrubs in British Columbia*. Vancouver: University of British Columbia, 1982.

Marchak, Patricia. *Green Gold: The Forest Industry in British Columbia*. Vancouver: University of British Columbia Press, 1983.

Ministry of Forests, British Columbia. Annual Reports: 1984/85, 1985/86, 1986/87, 1987/88, 1988/89, 1989/90, 1990/91, 1991/92, 1992/93, 1993/1994

Ministry of Forests, British Columbia. *Outdoor Recreation Survey 1989/90*. Victoria: Ministry of Forests, Recreation Branch, 1991.

Robson, Peter, ed. *The Westcoast Logger*. Vancouver: Westcoast Publishing. Volumes 1–3 (1990–93).

Schmidt, R.L. *The Silvics and Plant Geography of the Genus Abies in the Coastal Forests of British Columbia*. Victoria: British Columbia Forest Service, 1957.

Taylor, G.W. *Timber: History of the Forest Industry in B.C.* North Vancouver, BC: J.J. Douglas Ltd., 1975.

Wood, C.S. and G.A. Van Sickle. *Forest Insect and Disease Conditions: British Columbia and Yukon—1994*. Victoria: Natural Resources Canada, Canadian Forest Service, Pacific and Yukon Region, Pacific Forestry Centre, 1994.

Young, Cameron. *The Forests of British Columbia*. North Vancouver, BC: Whitecap Books, 1985.

INDEX